BRONZE AND IRON

BRONZE AND IRON

Old Latin Poetry from Its Beginnings to 100 B.C.

by JANET LEMBKE

UNIVERSITY OF CALIFORNIA PRESS

BERKELEY LOS ANGELES LONDON 1973

UNIVERSITY OF CALIFORNIA PRESS
BERKELEY AND LOS ANGELES, CALIFORNIA
UNIVERSITY OF CALIFORNIA PRESS, LTD.
LONDON, ENGLAND
COPYRIGHT © 1973 BY THE REGENTS OF
THE UNIVERSITY OF CALIFORNIA
ISBN: 0–520–02164–9
LIBRARY OF CONGRESS CATALOG CARD
NUMBER: 71–182274
PRINTED IN THE UNITED STATES OF AMERICA
DESIGNED BY DAVE COMSTOCK

TO HANS

yes

ACKNOWLEDGMENTS

Amicus certus in re incerta cernitur.
—Ennius, *Tragoediae* 216

Undoubted friends in a time of doubt are discovered, especially:

· Ada Bruce, Anna Blake, and Raymond White, teachers, whose love for English and the Classics was contagious;

· Felix Stefanile, poet, who first suggested that Old Latin could be made new again;

· D. S. Carne-Ross, editor of *Arion*, and his colleagues, who believed in this project before I did;

· Ruth Adams, reference librarian, who persuaded broody librarians in three states that books kept in stacks don't hatch;

· Anne D. Rosivach, who translated Alberto Grilli's scholarly Italian into unclotted English and said she enjoyed the work;

· The National Translation Center, which granted me a fellowship that was transformed without difficulty into books and time;

· and the Camenae.

Thank you.

Gratia habetur utrisque, illisque tibique simitu.
—Lucilius, 1092

Permission from the following to quote copyrighted material is gratefully acknowledged:

Harper & Row, Publishers: lines from "The Practical Sense" from *The Ordeal of Change* by Eric Hoffer, copyright © 1963 by Eric Hoffer.

Alfred A. Knopf, Inc.: six-line excerpt from "The Idea of Order at Key West" from *The Collected Poems of Wallace Stevens*, copyright © 1954 by Wallace Stevens.

Richard Lewis: poem by Lynette Joass from *Miracles: Poems by Children of the English-speaking World*, collected by Richard Lewis, published by Simon and Schuster, copyright © 1966 by Richard Lewis.

The Macmillan Company: excerpts from *The Mind of Primitive Man* by Franz Boas, copyright 1938 by The Macmillan Company.

W. W. Norton & Company, Inc. and Routledge & Kegan Paul Ltd.: excerpts from *Play, Dreams and Imitation in Childhood* by Jean Piaget, translated by C. Gattegno and F. M. Hodgson.

Charles Scribner's Sons: excerpts from *Feeling and Form* by Suzanne K. Langer, copyright 1953 by Charles Scribner's Sons.

American Weave, vol. 31, no. 2 (December 1967): "Waking intuitively . . . ," after Q. Lutatius Catulus, and "The Voice of Claudia." The latter appears in this MS in somewhat altered language and shape.

Arion: 6.3 (Autumn 1967): "R," "The Pioneers," "Epitaph" (Naevius), "Tattoo," "Ironstorm," "Victory," and "The Night Watch."

——: 7.2 (Summer 1968): "The West," "Portrait, Perhaps, of an Elder Poet," "All That Glitters" (in this MS called ". . . On the Nature of My Art"), and "Hymn for Seedtime and a Safe Harvest."

——: 7.4 (Winter 1968): "Waking intuitively . . . ," "Reveille," "Possessions" (in this MS called ". . . A Georgic"), "Epitaph" (Ennius), and "Toward Translation of an Ancient and Unimportant Soundstatement by Valerius Aedituus."

Felix and Selma Stefanile: "Clocks," after Aquilius, from *Duo*, poems by Janet Lembke and Morton Felix, Vagrom Chapbooks, Copyright October 1966, by Felix and Selma Stefanile. This *plasma* appears in this MS in very slightly different form.

SUMMARY OF
✑CONTENTS

READINGS OF HISTORY

- Do they show a typical development of the poem as an instrument of service to small group, large group or state, and individual in that chronological order?
- Do they illustrate the maturation of the poetic impulse from numinous nape-prickle to wholly intentional act?

READINGS OF HISTORY

... *of historical narratives, one part is* historia *or system-atic fact-finding, another part* mythos *or fairytale, and another,* plasma *or plausible invention. And of these,* historia *is the exposition of certain events that are true and have occurred: Alexander's death by treacherously administered drugs in Babylon. And* plasma *deals with events that have not occurred but are similar, in the re-tailing, to real events: the hypotheses of comedies and mimes. And* mythos *is an exposition of events that have never occurred and are false: poet-fabricated tales about the genera of poisonous spiders and snakes spawned by the blood of Titans, and Pegasus leaping from the Gor-gon's head after her throat was cut, and Diomedes's com-rades turned into birds, Odysseus into a horse, Hecuba into a dog. . . .*

—*Sextus Empiricus,* Adversus Grammaticos, *263–264*

*1
HISTORIA

O LD LATIN POETRY looks, more than two thousand years later, like Humpty Dumpty after the irreversible accident. As a body of literature it is smashed; here lies decapitated epic, there a toothless fragment of archaic satire. Comedy has lost its fist, tragedy its power to mirror and purge. Only scattered, mostly unmatching shards are left, embedded in layers of later work. And though it's been a matter of many theses—examining these meager verbifacts for clues to Latin's evolution and Rome's, all the world's ologists and all the world's ographers have not put Humpty together again.

The earliest remains represent a preprecious bronze age of Latin beginning no later than the eighth century B.C. and ending abruptly in the mid-third century B.C. It was not a literate age, much less a literary one. Some of the undatable verses left are as old as Rome, which legend founds in 743 B.C. These remnants of spoken traditions, popular and sacred, were first transcribed, sometimes without comprehension of meaning, centuries after they agglomerated in hut or grove. They include such minor curiosities as proverbs and prophecies, prayers and table graces, a charm to cure gout, and a set of abracadabras for healing a sprain. The names of the singers lie in the same limbo as those of the originators of Mother Goose. Some of the singsongs could well have been hatched by that good grey bird:

Hiberno pulvere, verno luto,
grandia farra, camille, metes.

—quoted by Macrobius, *Saturnalia,* V.20[1]

Winter of dust, spring of mud—
then reap, novice farmer, a good grain yield.

Lalla, lalla, lalla:
i, aut dormi aut lacta.

—quoted by the scholiast on Persius, 3.18[2]

Lullay, lullay, lullay:
either sleep, child, or suckle.

And here's the gout charm, lines that might have been sung
by an ancestor of the sorcerer's apprentice. It apparently in-
vokes some sort of gout spirit.

Ego tui memini,
medere meis pedibus:
terra pestem teneto,
salus hic maneto
in meis pedibus.

—quoted by Varro, *Rerum Rusticarum,* I.ii.27

I call on you,
now mend my big toe:
may earth soak up my pain,
here let good health remain
in my big toe.

Such little verses share Latin poetry's antique dark, in
which there is life but not volitional art, with the crude thump-
ing spring hymns of two priestly fraternities, the equinox-
greeting Salians and the Arval Brothers whose job it was to
pray for fertile soil and unblighted harvests. How old are the
songs? As old as Rome's legendary eighth-century founding?

Or older, composed perhaps during the settled seasons between the southward spilling treks of the Latin tribes down the Italian boot in the first millennium B.C.? One factual statement can be made. Some of the godnames in the hymns are abstractions for the sown earth and the stored harvest and thus show that these were the songs of an agricultural people rather than hunters or nomadic herdsmen.

The dark breaks suddenly. The iron age, the first formal age of Latin poetry, began with an amazing precision of date and author. The birthyear was 240 B.C.; the month, September; the occasion, the Roman Games made especially lavish in celebration of Rome's victory over Carthage in the First Punic War. (Morning or afternoon? Was it sunny?) Delivery occurred in the form of two plays, a comedy and a tragedy, employing Greek plots and meters. Their author-translator was the Greek freedman Livius Andronicus (284?–204? B.C.), who also composed hymns and recast the *Odyssey* into Latin saturnians for use as a teaching text. Saturnians were an Italic meter that, unlike Greek, was probably accentual rather than dependent on quantity and pitch. Livius's hymns are lost; fewer than a hundred lines from his *Odyssey* and some of the plays survive. Succeeding Livius, steadily excelling him, are a host of poets known, if they are known today at all, as dim totemic figures, the almost mythic ancestors of the great tribes of Western poets and playwrights: Naevius, dramatist and epic poet; Plautus, comic playwright; Ennius, man of all forms, the first Roman to climb Helicon and rape the Muses and carry them home like Sabine women; Pacuvius, tragic playwright; Caecilius, writer of comedies; Terence, comic playwright of great eloquence and elegance; Lucilius, Ur-satirist; Lutatius Catulus and Porcius Licinus and Valerius Aedituus, epigrammatists all and critics in meter; Accius, tragic playwright; Lucretius, philosopher; and others, named and nameless, the makers of dramatic, erotic, and didactic verses. Many of their surviving poems look like uninspired wordcarvings fashioned at dawn's light in imitation of Greek dreams. The shiny newness is quite gone now; lacunae riddle the lines like grubholes. The allusions ignite no modern associations and the events recalled have been made unreal by time's passing. But the iron poems greatly influenced the syntax and spelling of classical Latin and were the first significant vehicles for the entry of Greek words into the Latin language (and from it into English). And the work of contemporary poets as different in manner as Ezra Pound, Robert Lowell, and Louis Zukofsky trace iron contours at a single remove, that of translation from classical Latin. The iron age ended as abruptly as it began, on the eve of Catullus's (84–54 B.C.) initial attempt at poem.

There are exceptions to the rule of fragment, bronze or iron. The durability of inscribed stone and metal has kept intact some short poems—dedications, epitaphs, the Arval Hymn. Some of the comedies of Plautus (254–184 B.C.) and Terence (195–159? B.C.) have been handed down in reasonably uncorrupted manuscripts, as has the *de Rerum Natura* of Lucretius (98?–55 B.C.). These, however, lie outside the urbs of present consideration partly because of their accessibility in translations and partly because playwriting and philosophy have become creative modes now largely separated from poetry. In the case of the plays, translations are not only printed but physical, on stage or screen; the 1963 musical comedy *A Funny Thing Happened on the Way to the Forum* was a sometimes very close adaptation of Plautine material. To apply, moreover, the plastic kind of translation I think mandatory in dealing with the fragments as poetry to either Lucretius or the comedies would be like setting Claude Lévi-Strauss's anthropological materials into hexameters or rewriting W. C. Fields's dialogue in iambic senarii; it could—with dreadful effort—be done, but it's not worth trying.

The most powerful iron poems are now mutilated beyond restoration to any semblance of original wholeness. The epic *Annals* of Ennius once consisted of eighteen books of hexameters; it is now a ruin of fewer than six hundred lines and phrases, less than half a book, perhaps a fortieth of the whole. Lucilius wrote thirty books of satires; fewer than thirteen hundred lines and scraps of lines are left. The saturnian rubble of the earliest known national epic, *The Song of the Punic War* by Naevius, consists of only sixty-six probable excerpts. When a complete poem, usually short, or a passage of more than three consecutive lines survives, it seems a happy fluke, like finding a whole dinosaur egg in a literary Gobi.

How satisfying it would be to explain the survival of any Old Latin poetry by a law of natural literary selection. The initial loss of much iron poetry probably followed almost directly upon the last scratch of the poet's stylus. Though poetry was written down, it was in essence a performing art to be chanted and danced or acted or simply recited. In those years without commercial publishers and libraries, demands for copies would be brought about by enormous and immediate success in the popular ear, as with Plautus's comedies, or by schoolroom need. Even those works that passed popularity tests were subject to a stern and prudish government censorship. Unacceptable works were suppressed; there was small chance then for them to sleep for a hundred years and wake at the kiss of a discovery that they were neglected classics. But for some of the lucky passages that escaped this kind of annihilation, a principle of fitness does seem to be at work. In spite of the inherent fragility of ancient book materials and the equally inherent frailties of men—copyists will make mistakes, scholiasts embrace one-upmanship—some passages have been time-selected for their once and always poetry as worthy of continued life. Some of the best, however, have certainly been done in by uncontrollable natural forces—fire and flood and ordinary processes of decay. And some by human forces just as uncontrollable—barbarians destroying whatever did not glitter, crusaders rampant, Christians rejecting dirty stories, critics. Many lines reflect as the operative reason for present existence nothing more than taste, either the fancy of an individual or the groupthink of a generation. Some reveal the persistence not of intrinsic excellence but of the type of conservative pedagogy that today demands memorization of "Trees" and sets it up as a model poem: If it was good enough for your grandfather, it's good enough for you. Others owe preservation to similarly apoetic criteria: an elevated moral tone or sideshow peculiarities of language.

Cicero (106–43 B.C.) exemplifies the man concerned with moral tone. His letters and orations are meaty with quotations illustrating what he found eloquent in diction and admirable for sentiment. Luckily he was a gourmet. Here is a prose approximation of the words of Ulysses on his deathbed, from Pacuvius's tragedy *Niptra*:

> It is decent only to complain of bad luck, not lament it;
> this is man's duty. Tears are the genius of a woman.
> —*Tusculanae Disputationes*, II.21.50[3]

More often the lines have been fossilized in the useful but poetically meaningless works of the gourmandizers—the grammarians, the antiquaries, the archaizers. Though their volumes are unwitting Hesperiae of iron poetry, their motives for compilation had little to do with art and aesthetics. Instead, from the first century B.C. on, these writers nibbled at the poems with the bookworm zeal of starving anti-Muses and digested them for nonstandard orthography and obsolete word usages and archaic definitions—the hows of language rather than its whys. A prime source of such fragments, and typical of them, is the grammar of Nonius (fl. A.D. 300). He wrote, for example (468.20): "*Danunt* is the same as our *dant* [they give]. Naevius in the fourth book of *The Punic War* says, 'that meat they give to the victors.'" And (217.12): "We usually speak of the word *postica* [posterior, hind] in the feminine gender. Lucilius in his third book says, 'she hasn't given birth; the truth is, from her hind part she poured out . . .'"[4]

Such excisions pique curiosity. Is Ulysses's deathspeech a translation from Pacuvius's now-lost Sophoclean model, an adaptation, or an outright invention? What were the allusive ramifications for a non-Greek audience? What real or legendary occasion did Naevius fold into saturnians? Who are "they?" Who the victors? And who poured out whom or what? (Sounds like that old multipara, the Mother of Waters.)

The quoters themselves may not have known all the answers; many of their texts were corrupt. Future discoveries may resolve a few such problems of literal and historical import, but grasping at solutions to most of them will remain a task for Tantalus or the most relentlessly dedicated scholar.

For people interested in poetry such questions need no answers. Only two questions are worth asking. Do the remains of Old Latin tell anything about poetry, its beginnings and growing pains? And, in our day of moonflights and warfare limited by the threat of atomic holocaust and personal anguish generated by an impersonal megatechnocracy, can a few lines about shields and wolfsuckled twins be considered poetry of any contemporary relevance? In other words, how and why did the verses work? Can they work now?

The mere survival of the verses and the fact that once upon an elder time they were accepted as poetry hardly warrant new English versions nor yet another explication of their history. But in explications past the remains of Old Latin poetry have been treated peripherally as clues to the growth of a language and a nation, as simpleminded forebears of the great classical poems, or as wordpictures characterizing the Roman of the Republic. Their central fact of being—their poetry—has been vastly ignored. Enough, however, is left to suggest a general route, with peculiarly Roman hazards, for the poet's journey from magician to maker and to trace a specific pattern for the growth of his sense of creative responsibility for his work. Enough is left to illustrate a sure shift of emphasis within the poem itself from sheer creature survival in the certain maw of death to illumination of the possibilities of life. And there's something about Old Latin poetry that can't be circumscribed by calendar and artifact and geography, something immune to changing tastes: man's recognition of man.

2
MYTHOS

WHEN SEXTUS EMPIRICUS, the skeptic philosopher, divided history as written in his time into three parts, he used the word *mythos* to describe the kind of narration that he found to be wholly without factual basis and, therefore, false. Myth has come to mean something more. It's still a fabulous story, yes, but it is also seen as the result of human striving to explain things and happenings that undeniably exist or occurred but for which there is little or no factual information available.

Here, then, is a myth about Old Latin poetry.

Literature has its grain-of-truth old wives' tales. One of the hardiest—and hardest to sort out—is that Latin poetry sprang from nothingness into vital though slavish somethingness through a process in which Rome's headlong embrace of a roundly ripe Greek literature produced a glorious bastard. I think, however, that Greek art is rather to be viewed as sophisticated new clothing—bonebending swaddling, if you will —for an already squalling craft. As physical growth is not superimposed on the child but comes in response to internal signals, Latin poetry burgeoned in answer to local stimuli. Greece's splendid gifts were the formal techniques for handling that response, as schooling gives the child successively more complex tools with which to handle the data of expanding reality. It is imaginable, though futile to debate, that without Greek techniques the Latin craft would have been retarded or arrested forever at a point of youthful mediocrity. The bronze and iron poems are, I admit, often mediocre and sometimes very bad. Only occasionally do they touch greatness. But they are real poems. And it is absurd to say that Latin poetry did not have a life of its own before Greek techniques entered poetic practice. Nor could the techniques have been adopted if the Roman poets had not already outgrown their craft and inwardly matured enough to need and seize and use them. It has often been remarked in disparaging terms that the Romans were not innovative geniuses. What has not been especially noted is that they were outstanding adaptive geniuses who could take the innovations of others—in engineering and military skills, most prominently—and put them to larger, thoroughly Roman uses.

But the baby is still cocooned and faceless in the arms of the gossips. What were the practices of bronze poetry? What conditions within and without the Latin poets' physical selves informed these practices? What local signals of body and history brought the poets to their iron instar? *Why?* What bronze practices endured, and how?

My myth is drawn in part from the chronology itself of the remnants attributable to the centuries in question. There are bronze remains of both poetry and law. All the poetic fragments, bronze and iron, can be treated both as art and—Emerson's phrase—"archives of history" pointing to historical conclusions. The myth receives some detail from later Latin authors—poets, rhetoricians, grammarians, biographers, a historian—who investigated the putative origins of some poetic forms in Latium or recorded and sometimes commented on elder passages or made hindsighted critical pronouncements on the nature and rules of poetry. Finer shadings are added by modern studies in the humanities and sciences and those hybrids that apply scientific method to artistic intuition. Then, speculation provides some highlights. For guesses and opinions, no apologies. The myth is not to be seen as the work of a scholar's cool documentary hand. It is meant rather as a history in essence, an on-off-on stroboscopic suggestion of environments for the poems as art.

> *He in whom there is not any art is called inert.*
> —Lucilius, 474[5]

It will be helpful to take a ball of thread—some articles of faith—into the Roman maze. What is poetry as an art? What, in the first place, is art? (Will people ever agree on definitions? Can paragraphs succeed where volumes have failed?) Let's use some mid-twentieth-century ideas. They are controversial, but they provide the broad terms on which this exploration of Old Latin poetry is based.

The philosopher Suzanne Langer says, "Art is the creation of forms symbolic of human feeling." And, on poetry's core of being, "The poet's business is to create the appearance of 'experiences,' the semblance of events lived and felt, and to organize them so they constitute a purely and completely experienced reality, a piece of *virtual life.*" That is to say, the poem does not recount a truth; it *makes* one. Poetry differs from other forms of art through its use of words; and it differs from other verbal modes through its devices. On poetry's source or inspiration and its function, Mrs. Langer says, ". . . we are driven to the symbolization and articulation of feeling when we *must* understand it to keep ourselves oriented in society and nature."[6]

Remarkably ecumenical definitions. They shelter equally all poetic themes and types and styles and any tricks that any poet has adopted or discovered to set his work apart from other poetries and unpoetries. The schools and isms are reconciled. Yet, there's room for changes of emphasis and techniques within poetry, and we can see those extremes of age-old argument—Dionysius and Apollo, redskins and palefaces—as cells coexisting in the same body. The ghosts of Stevens and Eliot share Elysium impartially with the leaping shade of a Salian hymnshouter.

A few words more on poetry's source-and-function. . . .
A need for orientation posits *dis*orientation. The existence of
a stress situation. It has recently been persuasively suggested
by the poet and critic Stanley Burnshaw that poetry—indeed
all creative effort, artistic and scientific—is a phenomenon
resulting from biological necessity, the human body's physical
need to unburden itself of accumulated, intolerable stress.[7]
This idea is given weight by the biologists. Seymour Levine, a
developmental and behavioral neuroendocrinologist, has ana-
lyzed bodily response to stress in terms of pituitary-adrenal
system stimulation caused by somatic or psychological insults
—a burn, a loud thunderclap, "mere exposure to a novel en-
vironment." This bodily response is designed for physical
protection. It includes increased electrical activity in the brain,
a rise in the levels of certain hormones in the blood, and some
noticeable motor activity; interestingly, Pavlov called this
busy-ness an "orientation reflex."[8] Here may well be the
physiological basis for the quick spinetingles, hair bristling
on the nape of the neck, the goosebumps, the sudden feeling
of constriction in the chest that can be experienced on hearing
a song, reading a poem, perceiving something old and familiar
in a new light. And here, I suspect, is the answer to the hoary
question of what a flash of "inspiration" really is. Most of us
become physically habituated to a psychological stress that is
repeated over and again. An artist, a scientist, an innovative or
adaptive thinker is perhaps then someone whose habituation
mechanism remains in some respect immature, who stays as
open as a child to novelty. Physiology may also supply some
answers to questions about the rhythms expected in poetry—
that they are based on the body's natural rhythms, such as
heartbeat, pulse, the circadian cycle. And also to questions
about the source of inspiration that Aristotle called *manikē*,
manic ecstasy (*Poetics*, 1455a.33–34): a body under stress
may alter adrenalin to adrenochrome, a substance chemically
similar to the active principle in mescaline.[9] I do not mean to
imply, however, that a *poem* is a product of the pituitary-
adrenal system, the pulse, and hormone conversion. "Inspira-

tion"—a reflex, a reaction—is void unless it is acted upon. The poet must collaborate with inspiration; only after his words are spoken or written can they become an artifact. And the artifact itself does not fully exist as poem until it is so perceived by a hearer or reader.

How are artifacts put forth as poetry to be judged as good art or bad, major or minor, or no art at all? To the extent, I think, that they re-inspire the reader-hearer and, much more important—even if the reader-hearer is not re-inspired and does not feel the physical symptoms described above—that they are understood as valid resolutions of orientation-need in the context of their making. Whenever—now, the nineteenth century, the eighth century B.C. And the context can include history, physical environment, culture, frames of mind, whatever is needed to bring about understanding. Some of the Latin fragments are almost impossible for us to perceive as poetry because their contexts are nearly or completely lost. They can be admired only for technical reasons, such as meter, or for the light they shed on matters of history. Some old lines, however, can be resurrected; these are the good ones that meet us halfway if we just spend a little effort putting them in context. Still other poems transcend their loci in time; these are the great ones—the *Iliads*—that pull us into them, even though their references, their ideas, may be quite alien. They are accessible, they invite us, through the humanity we hold in common with the man who wrote and the men he wrote about.

One poem may of course hold contradictions. Part of it may vitally symbolize feeling; part may simply vanish as art. But, as the satirist Lucilius wrote in the second century B.C., ". . . no one who finds fault with Homer finds fault continuously or with the *oeuvre* . . . he finds fault with a verse, a word, a piece of reasoning, or a passage" (408–410). The Old Latin fragments are a hodgepodge of goodness, badness, and mediocrity, but, as has been mentioned, their preservation is due at least as much to reasons of personal and scholarly utility as to aesthetic ones. Iron badness, moreover, played a necessary gritty part in bringing Latin to its classical polish.

Bad and good, the balance of parts decides the poem's leverage, its power to move creator and receiver toward satisfaction of their mutual need for orientation, an inner need as urgent and involuntary as the body's demands for air and food and sleep.

I find three chief and historically coeval, though not always discrete, varieties of bronze and iron poetry. They can be distinguished one from another by the kind of orientation-need that generated them, by imputation of creative impulse, and by human reception. That is, by the poet's awareness of his role as the agent of symbol, whatever variety or combination he used; by the degree of his active collaboration with inspiration; and by the purposes to which the poems were put. The evolution to be traced is triple-track, not a one-thread chronological progression from technically simple bronze poems to more complex, Greek-influenced ones. Such an investigation would result in another literary history of the fads and fashions that successively dressed Old Latin poetry's essential, art-defining symbolic effectiveness. In this effectiveness there was no change, no progression. Where poetry exists at all, its source-and-function is constant. The Roman changes that did occur as time passed seem rather to have been ones of the poets' growing overt participation in making a poem and of the poem's emphasis on the kind of man-world relationships for which poetry found symbols. For simplicity's sake, I'll refer to the three varieties as the poetries of survival, celebration, and possibility. It may be worthwhile to mention again that the practice of poetry, bronze and iron, was the practice of a performing art. Words joined music and movements, or they were recited, and either way, poetry was simply the spoken vehicle of feeling in a grand conglomerate form created for ears, eyes, noses, and jostled bodies.

The first variety, the poetry of survival, is a creature plea for life in a world of humanly ungovernable circumstances. And it is an expression of the bonds of bodily necessity that link men to the elemental forces that both threaten and sustain them. It deals with the natural world and inhuman events, lightning and equinox and the earth's yearly regeneration. It says, Men are alike because their physical environment is the same and shared. Though it originates in a single person, it is characterized by group acceptance, group transmission, and reception by the ageless human longing to eliminate the things that go bump in the night. Its tone is the tone of hopeful, fearful people approaching a mystery. Its tense is an eternal present—what is, has always been and always shall be. It was used magically, sacramentally, and once accepted, it was immutable. Its then-and-now nameless authors or agglomerators —prophets and priests admitting no internal creative force— assigned responsibility for the poem's being to a Muse or other extrahuman source. The bronze hymns, the oldest extant Latin poems, furnish examples. Automatic writing, hallucinogenic write-ins, and found poetry might be considered contemporary analogues, though in found poetry the Muse is often ultimately detectible as Madison Avenue or a menu-maker or a state traffic commission. There is a curious correspondence between found poem and bronze counterpart: the presenter of found poems takes words externally given and passes them on as a sometimes rearranged but not revised expression of the unease his manmade but uncontrollable environment stirs in him. And with hybris he signs his name!

The poetry of celebration rises in one man's voluntary acceptance of a social challenge to commemorate and weave into general experience the recurring, inevitable events of biology and the great events of man's own making—birth, death, marriage, war and triumph. At first it is a sacred poetry because the matters with which it deals are holy to primitive people. It attempts to create a stable relationship, a quick reference between the singular human occasion and its past and future collective counterparts, and it appeals to a group awareness of matters as large as national identity, as pettily pervasive as the wish to immortalize oneself in epitaph. It is a poetry of culture, the manmade world, and it says, We are alike because our biological processes and our society are the same. It is a poetry of large statements. Once experimentation has established an ideal tone, this poetry becomes conservative, past-looking, sometimes to the point of being antiexperimental. Its present tense is often the historical present. In Rome it was quickly formalized as a solemn, adult, and intellectual poetry often used institutionally by government and schools to reinforce values considered socially desirable or to perpetuate a teacher's idea of a good thing. Bronze examples exist in epitaphs; the most prominent iron examples are those of Naevian and Ennian epic. A modern poem such as Robert Frost's "The Gift Outright" serves to suggest the not infrequent nobility of Old Latin intent.

The poetry of possibility is the poetry of anything-goes. The last variety to appear full-grown in Rome, it is one man's deliberate shaping of his orientation-need and unique emotional experiences into words charged with conveying abstractions of such heart's ideas as love, despair, hate, friendship, and plain cranky feelings of having gotten up on the wrong side of bed. It is supremely a poetry of opinion and is designed to be sent home as a one-to-one message straight into the self-consciousness (or conscience) of another person. It is the poetry of man's inner world, and it says, I am not like you. It goads. It invites argument or agreement. It uses the sudden, small, nuclear insight to turn ordinary perceptions of reality topsy-turvy. It always seeks new technical possibilities. Its present tense refers to the here and now but can suggest courses for possible future action as well. And it is by far the most difficult variety of Old Latin poetry to translate because the puns don't work in English, the jokes aren't funny anymore, and the allusions are understandable through an academic rather than immediate grasp of connotations. Its references to the poet's private life, real people otherwise unrecorded, and tiny events can overwhelm symbolic content unless some sort of contemporary correspondence can be found. The dinner guest who won't go home—we know him too; heartbreak—we've felt it. This quality of seeming temporality, of momentariness, may well account for the fact that no bronze examples have been saved. But there are enough later references to bronze practice to allow a few deductions. In the iron satires the poetry of possibility finds a true if rusty voice. Does it need contemporary illustration?

And now for contexts.

BRONZE

From Neolithic Times to Mid-fifth Century B.C.

Hear the voice of the Bard!
Who Present, Past, & Future sees;
Whose ears have heard
The Holy Word
That walk'd among the ancient trees,

Calling the lapsèd Soul,
And weeping in the evening dew;
That might control
The starry pole
And fallen light renew!

'O Earth, O Earth, return!
Arise from the dewy grass;
Night is worn
And the morn
Rises from the slumbrous mass.

'Turn away no more;
Why wilt thou turn away?
The starry floor,
The wat'ry shore
Is giv'n thee till the break of day.'

—William Blake, *Songs of Experience*

Who shaped the Holy Word for Mediterranean ears? Formless sensation, shiver of inspiration, a power, an unseen leaf-rustling presence, a divine being personifying originative impulse? At the behest of ecstasy Orpheus the magician sang the trees and stones to dance. The Muses came down from their mountaintops to grant insight to Homer singing in the grove of his blindness; they came down and placed an olive branch in Hesiod the shepherd's hand to signify his divine commission to make poetry. And well into iron times the Camenae whispering like oak leaves, bubbling like springs, told their secrets to Roman ears.

Muses, Camenae, who or what are they? The words seem freely convertible because they perform an identical service in embodying poem's originative impulse. Identity, however, ends there. Each bevy tells its own version of the nature of an art that began before there was a notion of Muse. The classical Muses are to be associated with poetic practices—resolutions of need, that is—in a phase of creative responsibility greater than that represented by the wild Italian Camenae. The former, as those relatively tame ladies are met in the oldest Greek poetry, have already become divinities as idealized in function as later Periclean sculpture was in form. At the turn of the first millennium B.C., the invocations in *Iliad* and *Odyssey* neither name nor number the Muses, but they have by this time emerged from neuter formlessness. They are gynemorphs inhabiting mountain heights. They are the beautiful, fitful, jealous, cruel, and holy daughters of Zeus who give or withhold the power of poetry in response to invocations that express not passion but routinely reverent good manners. By the eighth century Hesiod invoked them generally as "Pierian Muses" at the outset of his *Works and Days* and listed in his *Theogony* (77–79) the nine daughters of Zeus and Memory by the names today most familiar: Clio and Euterpe, Thalia, Melpomene and Terpsichore and Erato and Polyhymnia and Urania and Calliope. The Muse-idea was known in Greece by other names; Pausanias, the Baedeker-Fodor-Temple Fielding of the second century A.D., records the existence of an old Boeotian triad in his *Description of Greece* (IX.xxix.2): Melete, Mneme, and Aoide, whom translation undisguises as Practice, Memory, and Song. Though Hesiod did not link his Muses to specific spheres of responsibility, their names alone indicate that the ladies had begun to specialize. Terpsichore "delighted in the dance"; Clio, later to be history's inseparable companion, even then "proclaimed" or "celebrated." In addition to adhering to the convention of invoking the Muses, both Homer and Hesiod may truly have believed that inspiration was born of divinity, that an extrahuman agency helped to create poem from initial impulse, and that a vocation to poetry was a sign that the gods did especially love them. But their works and the Muse-names suggest that they also held themselves accountable for their accomplishments, for craftsmanship and content.

Was Homer a grand redactor who represented the end of Greek oral tradition? As such did he plump an inborn gift for overall narrative recollection by drawing on a professional heritage of catalogues and similes and memory-joggers such as epithets designed by gender and case to fit the established metrical scheme of epic song? For, Homeric epic represents a matured form. Or, did Homer stand at the beginnings of written literature in Greece as sole inventor and revisor of his words, though not of his form? This quarrel belongs to the experts. It has no importance in speculating on the degree of his overt participation in the creative act. To deny Homer literacy is not to deny him the deliberate selection of material. It is important that he was named. Were he one man or several, again let the experts debate; his quantity is irrelevant. As a named composer, the man—not a Muse—was marked for praise, damnation, or yawns for what was sung and how it was sung. Were Homer oral editor or dictating author, he was certainly one of a proud body, a singers' guild of indeterminably prehistoric origin. Its members were schooled and then, having lasted the course of apprenticeship, were allowed, unlike the Salian priests, to break and harness the willful Muses with hard-earned skills until age or death put an end to their singing. And, editor or author, the guildsinger Homer was not averse to giving his Muses a nudge. He employed the techniques that years of Practice had given him. He sorted Memory's fund of plots and unified his selections into intricate tales of his own design. And, working within the strait discipline of the matured epic form, he made a Song. Divinely commissioned, humanly trained singers hold prominent and dramatic roles in Homeric epos. In the *Iliad* the bard Thamyris boasts of his abilities, only to forfeit both them and his sight to Muses angered at his arrogance; Achilles's godwrought, kinetic shield resounds with lyres and flutes and inspired bardic song. In the *Odyssey* Agamemnon, on the eve of departure for the Trojan War, entrusts Clytemnestra's shakable virtue to his court poet's guardianship; Odysseus is entertained by the "godlike musician" Demodocus in the palace hall of King Alcinous, while faraway in his own hall on Ithaca "inspired" and "trusty" Phemius is forced from loyal silence to song by the too-ready swords of Penelope's squatter suitors. These poets-cum-showmen were attended by glamour, admiration, an aura of holiness, and peril (inspiration's attendance is open to question). The *Odyssey*'s bards may serve as models of the guildsinger. They performed a double labor of skill and necessity. For, the pursuit of poetry was an employment; it was a means to livelihood as well as to resolution of orientation-need. Surely Demodocus sang not just to answer Calliope, soothe Alcinous, and entertain Odysseus but literally for his supper. However beloved and honored, however self-convinced that a power of external origin infused him, such a poet must have spent long hours responding with song to nothing more inspiring than a patron's undivine commission to make a little music to dine and drink by. And, during the years of Odysseus's absence, Phemius was inspired by no poetic stimulus; a gut fear of death, should he refuse to perform, thrust the lyre into his hands and put songs in his mouth. The show must go on. Techniques consciously acquired but polished and made automatic by much use filled Demodocus's belly and kept Phemius's head attached to his neck.

Hesiod was not a guildsinger but an apparently self-taught peasant of strong didactic bent. Two centuries after Homer he acknowledged his own sense of creative responsibility —as well as taking a bluestocking's swipe at Homer's recording of unedifying behavior in heaven—when he wrote that though the Muses speak truthfully when they wish, they may also speak falsehood as if it were truth (*Theogony*, 26–28). The poet's task was in part to separate golden words from gilded ones. That is, to exercise choice.

Thus, in Greece, half a millennium before Aristotle (384–322 B.C.) named the sources of poetry as manic madness or a happy natural gift (*Poetics*, place cited), the latter—enhanced by training and careful selection of material—governed poetic composition. Homer and Hesiod were voluntary celebrators who sought rationally to entertain and inform. Though a poet's work might be characterized as charming and enchanting, adjectives that look back to Orpheus and magic, the Greek word ποιητής (poet) means "maker" and connotes action-moving purposefully ahead rather than reaction-waiting for the Muses' stimulation and then responding to it. The Muses as poem's sharp and ecstatic seminal event, as found words and phrases from the blue, as swift insights, were naturally in no way denied by the Greeks. But as such they were incorporated into the greater poem rather than providing its totality.

The Roman Camenae were another cauldron of witches.

THE POETRY OF SURVIVAL: ITS ROMAN MAKING

Those whom men speak of as Muses are not the Camenae.

—Ennius, *Spuria?* 43

Many of the bronze Latin verses now in existence—lulla-by, goutsong, hymns—are *carmina* of the Camenae or, literally, charms of the chantresses. As prehistoric source-representatives of poetry, these immaterialities were, like other primeval Roman spirits, sexless and nameless *numina*, the externalized abstractions of human feeling. It was they from whom words flowed glossolaliac into men's mouths. With the gradual intro-duction of anthropomorphism at least as early as the eighth century B.C. from Greek-influenced Etruria to the north and Magna Graecia in southern Italy, they assumed femininity and two-three-four shapes in the Roman imagination. The collective name and separate natures of these spirits signify the arrival of

Latin poetry's three streams at the brink of the alphabet. The Camenae were not to be widely equated with the Muses before the beginning of the iron period in 240 B.C., when Greek practice—poet as willing collaborator—took over the making of Latin poetry, nor did the Muses begin to displace them until fifty more years had passed. The first Muse-cult at Rome was founded in 187 B.C. by M. Fulvius Nobilior, the patron of the epic poet Ennius. Did the Camenae have preclassical relatives in Greece between the times of Orpheus the magician and Homer the maker? Probably.

The Camena now best known was Egeria, nymph of spring and grove. Mythographers have identified her as mistress-councillor to Numa Pompilius (traditionally 715–672 B.C.), legend's successor to King Romulus. Numa was credited by later Romans with the institution, on Egeria's divine and trystworthy advice, of the oldest laws and religious observances and with the invention of a calendar for keeping track of religion's seasonal cycle. He was also thought to have been the first chanter of the Salian hymns, supposedly burbled in his ears by his lady of the fountain (or source). The second, and simultaneously third and fourth, Camena was Carmenta. Her prime name states her gift for song (*carmen*) and perhaps for wisdom (*Mens*, or mind personified as the goddess of wisdom). And as if these intangible gifts were not enough to have admitted her to Camenahood, the Romans believed that she had brought them a visible admission ticket, the alphabet. Carmenta on occasion split herself into Postvorta and Antevorta, personifications of foresight and hindsight, or appeared in combination with them as a trinity. She was the Roman version of the "Present, Past, & Future" seen by Blake's bard, who is a vatic singer bloodclose to the bronze Romans and only distantly kin to the Homeric guildsingers.

Now, the Romans being notoriously possessed of near-fetched imaginations that spun legends close to truth, these names and identities only lightly veil what I think were real poetic practices and restrictions affecting the now-extant Latin verse most ancient in origin, the survival hymns of the Salians and Arval Brothers. However the modern mythologists interpret the Numa-Egeria relationship—Gravesian thesis of black poplar death goddess[10] swatting her poor doomed creature with a club of fearful rapture or *Golden Bough* explanation of it as the sweetly romantic storyfication of ritual vegetation-regenerating sex between oak-queen and king of the wood[11]—it seems to have clear politicoreligious implications. (Which came first, chicken or egg, politics or religion?) The story can be read as an allegory justifying the prehistoric reservation to a ruling priestly hierarchy of the use and transmission of words that expressed what was *sacer*—right and holy or, equally, unlawful and cursed. These priests were qualified for their offices by patrician birth. Almost certainly, in keeping with the spirit-ridden times, they believed themselves externally inspired, numinously commissioned voices. And were Carmenta once a regional name for a matriarchal triple goddess[12] or, later, the convenient disembodiment of the alphabet's forgotten human sources, as Camena she marks Latin poetry's first wobbly step into literacy and literature: hierarchical recognition that the ABC's were potent, potentially dangerous knowledge best controlled as a religious mystery. The Word. This is not to say that only highborn priests knew their Latin letters but that they were much more likely to do so than other Romans. Carmenta's division into Postvorta and Antevorta explains the aim of control. From whatever real events the concept of the mirror-image twins arose—the weddings of flesh and blood virgins to sacred king and tanist; posterior-anterior or head-breech presentations of children at birth;[13] or new year's meeting of the past and the future—Carmenta in the guise of hindsight stood metonymically for close, historically attested priestly guardianship of the bronze records of law, commerce, religion, and history whether orally transmitted or inscribed on bark, linen, and oxhides; in the entrail-splattered robes of augury and foresight she represented drawing on these traditional materials to chant and prophesy and publish by mouth whatever rules were necessary to keep the people on their best behavior. The Law and its prophets. The reason that the priests controlled writing and literacy may have been that a spoken word believed to hold *numen* would itself become a numinous object when it was written. But sacred words or profane ones, the major effect of the near monopoly on writing was maintenance of political power through the promise of fostering social stability; the dangers to be avoided were paroxysmic social changes brought about by the rapid dissemination of information that writing and general literacy make possible. Under such circumstances the historic performers of the Salian and Arval hymns were men who considered themselves not poets but priests and prophets. Poetry for them was not an art in itself but a ceremonial adjunct of law and religion. The poem on their tongues no longer reflected the emotions born of a seminal event; it had become a numiniferous instrument of social conservation. And its function for them was to influence and order life magically rather than to illuminate and explain it poetically. That idea of "order" is best defined as superimposition of command and regulation. It was not a reduction of chaos from within.

But though the Camenae tell much about the bronze applications of survival poetry, they tell nothing about its making. The two hymns sprang, of course, from the human need for orientation to nature's inhuman events, and, as minor parts of increasingly more stylized ritual performances, they continued to serve, though less and less immediately, as necessary encapsulations of human feeling. The Salian hymns of equinox were created—when?—surely before the seventh century of Numa, if a king named Numa ever really reigned, and perhaps long before Rome's traditional founding in the eighth century. They were passed down the centuries like rumors, ancient words gathering garble, until the scholar Varro—first?—recorded some of them with all their encrusted, unintentional corruptions in the first century B.C. The less ancient but also corrupt Arval plea that earth be blightlessly fertile was still performed in the third century A.D., at least a thousand years after it was first made. The idea behind both hymns is as old as man's domestication of wild grain.

Again there are questions. Who made the hymns? What was the degree of voluntary participation in the making? How great was the belief in external inspiration, in a divine gift of song? And how, in the bronze centuries, was survival poetry practiced? It's impossible, barring the invention of a time machine, to answer these questions once and for all. But circumstantial evidence, classical and modern, licenses some poetic inconclusions.

> . . . the sanctuary . . . the holy secrets of the chief priest:
> though I never arrive at true knowledge of them, at least I
> may chase the wild goose of conjecture.
>
> —Varro, de Lingua Latina, V.i.8

To begin with, however, here are a few nonconjectural facts about the Salian priests. They are described by Greek and Roman writers and portrayed in sculpture and gem with enough detail to let imagination give them three dimensions and dress them and send them leaping into the jerky, percussive three-step that welcomed the equinoctial apparition of "the force that through the green fuse drives the flower."

During the month of March—beginning on the first, the Roman New Year— and again in October, twelve young male priests of Mars performed their rites. The purpose of the rites is not now entirely clear, but it is in part an honoring and placation of the Mars-*numen* that guarded both agriculture and war. For, March was the start of the growing and war seasons (in those days when war had a season), and October was the end. The priests wore caps with floppy peaks, bronze breastplates, embroidered thigh-high military tunics of antique, probably Italic design. In the right hand, each carried a short staff and on the left arm each bore a broad, torso-long shield shaped like a thick-waisted figure eight, a form no longer used in battle and so ancient that a legend of heavenly manufacture had been invented to explain its origin. The shape was actually derived from Crete and Mycenae. The rites must have been noisy affairs. Dancing through the streets, the Salians moved from station to ritually prescribed station and sang the hymns and thumped their staffs against the shields; the watchers along the way danced with them as they passed. The name of the priesthood comes from the nature of the dance; the verb *saliare* means to leap or jump. The priesthood is now thought to have been instituted in preurban Rome no later than the eighth century B.C. and it endured at least into the first century of the Christian era. Similar leaping societies existed in Italian towns other than Rome, and there are records of Greek analogues.

It may also be possible to give the Salians a fourth dimension—that of a particular kind of thought. Salian brains were sparked, I believe, by two examinable pressures: the external cultural dictates of an ancient social order and the body's internal promptings. As archaic Salian thought appears in the hymns, it seems to me to exhibit some of the elements of a highly logical primitive thinking and some of the characteristics of the child's prelogical thinking. Salian thought might be called a breccia in which the two modes are fragmentarily discernible but not able to be separated from each other nor lifted from the matrix of archaic thought in general.

Archaic thought: the primitive mindstyle as Camena

A general comparison of the primitive mindstyle to our domesticated one may make clear what the former is. I yield to men who have made primitive thought their business. More than half a century ago the anthropologist Franz Boas wrote:

> The first impression gained from a study of the beliefs of primitive man is, that while the perceptions of his senses are excellent, his power of logical interpretation seems to be deficient. I think it can be shown that the reason for this fact is not based on any fundamental peculiarity of the mind of primitive man, but lies, rather, in the character of the traditional ideas by means of which each new perception is interpreted; in other words, in the character of the traditional ideas with which each new perception

associates itself determining the conclusions reached. . . . The difference in the mode of thought of primitive man and that of civilized man seems to consist in the difference of the character of the traditional material with which the new perception associates itself. The instruction given to the child of primitive man is not based on centuries of experimentation, but consists of the crude experience of generations.[14]

This characterization is amplified by a contemporary anthropologist, Claude Lévi-Strauss. He uncovers the origin of the "traditional ideas": Men have from earliest times tackled a tough job—systematically organizing the data perceived by their senses. The reason for such organization is man's primordial need to resist chaos (to orient himself) by creating some sort of cosmos, even one based on what he is told by his eyes and ears and nose. And Lévi-Strauss finds that the differences between primitive and "scientific" thought reside not only in the character and transmittal of accumulated material; the modes are also distinguished by the kinds of phenomena with which they are involved and by the levels of reality to which they address themselves. The primitive mind looks at, say, lightning in terms of luck; the domestic mind may summon Ben Franklin. Then, where primitive thought often makes connections between its hunches and its final idea by means of intuition and imagination, domestic thought balks at such a leap and insists on testing and describing the connective steps. These differences, however, are more apparent than innate, and they do not point to inequalities in mental development. Both modes employ similar intellectual processes and comparable methods of study. For both, the world is a source of intellectual satisfaction as much as it is a resource for satisfying bodily needs. And all thought—ancient, modern, primitive, prelogical, domestic—drives toward identical goals: to create rational order and to gain objective knowledge.[15] Although thought attracts adjectives according to its application and aims, its nature is not subject to qualification, no matter where the operations of thought take place, Neolithic magician making celestial observations or scientist plotting a moon landing.

Technologically, the Latin people of the eighth century B.C. lived in the Iron Age. By then their tribes had been settled in Latium for perhaps two hundred years. The social and economic bases for life had been set by those acts of applied Neolithic imagination that discovered weeds could be tamed for a dependable food supply and wild animals gentled and bred for food, clothing, shelter, and transport, but the hilltop herding and farming villages of Latium had long left behind the hand-to-mouth dailiness of a completely primitive economy. The farmers who commuted to valley fields could raise two crops a year. Though the villagers had not yet dreamed a great city, in material matters they were caught in—and were contributing mightily to—that metamorphosis in Italy in which tribal generalism would give way to the diversifications of effort that would eventually support an empire. In spite of malarial marshes at the feet of the villages and water problems due to deforestation, the site of Rome-to-be possessed good potential for becoming an urban center. Geography made the site fortifiable. Its location near north-south land routes and its free access by way of the Tiber to the Mediterranean made it a natural marketplace and a magnet for people. Control of salt deposits near the Tiber's mouth fostered dependence in neighboring settlements. All of these factors made for real political clout.

But thought remained Neolithic. The inchworm effect was at work. For all the material progress altering and improving the lifestyle of the preurban, patriarchal, king-ruled tribes, their mindstyle, governed by grey-bearded ideas, had not yet looped forward from the stony past. The Latins seem to have been much like the people of Italy's Mezzogiorno today, who physically inhabit the twentieth century but whose minds are caught in a traditional mixture of medieval faith and pre-Christian superstition. The virtue of the traditional ideas—a common store of taught ancestral patterns of behavior and thought—was, and is, that they answer man's desire for order and comfort his need to be able to predict and control at least the human aspects of an existence continually battered by unpredictable, uncontrollable natural or thing-imposed changes. Their vice is that their conservation can become an end in itself rather than a means to species preservation. The traditional ideas of the Latin tribes preserved and perpetuated well into Republican times a social system that was removed by time and elaboration, but not in essence, from its primitive agricultural and pastoral archetype.

The members of the archetypal farming community that gave its social organization to the Latin villages were linked by bonds of aim and obligation undreamed of by the perpetrators of the Togetherness nightmare. The earliest farmers, like their primitive counterparts today, produced merely enough food for subsistence. And in the threat of famine only constant cooperation between man and man could ensure continuing life; men were the slaves of their hunger. The social system was the collective projection of each member's fundamental drive toward survival. There was no separation between church and state, or between religious life and daily life. Labor was generally divided according to age and sex. Adulthood arrived not with the toughening of muscles and the brittling of bones nor with the appearance of body hair and menstrual blood. It came, *e pluribus unum*, with the smooth seamless complete absorption of the fractious child-unit into the greater social unit. Under harsh life conditions of all or no one at all, the greater unit's strength lay in conformity. Unlike the members of hunting societies who tend to emphasize—and survive by—personal strength and prowess, who cherish eccentricity in dream and shaman, any cellular member of an early agricultural society who made continuing public expression of individuality had to be regarded as an unbearable, morbid infection in the social body. This is not to say there was no individuality; private lives held their own griefs and joys, A could sing a finer song than B, B was handsomer than A. The only public specialists such a system tolerated, however, were the keepers and self-perpetuating incarnations of its continuity, the priests, who were in the very beginning the chosen advisors of the king. (Who were in Latium themselves the kings and aristocracy.) They held, interpreted, and doled out objective knowledge that had been accumulated largely through imaginative, perceptive observations of those phenomena—thunderstorms and black frosts, bird migrations, the coruscating events of heaven— that impinged on agriculture and thus on the survival of the people. The simple bits of knowledge were strung together to make two kinds of connections between the community and its environment, and the uses of these connections gave the priests considerable secular as well as sacred power, for they could control food supplies and distribution.

The first connection was practical. It was employed for visible future ends. Without being able to explain cause and effect relationships between, for example, equinox and warming soil or warmth and germination, the priests nonetheless effectively directed planting for the future benefit of everyone. The same kind of practical connection can be seen in herbal medicine and the familiar weather jingle,

> Red sky at night, sailor's delight.
> Red sky in the morning, sailor take warning.

and in the Latin gnome about a dusty winter and a wet spring (an unlikely reversal, by the way, of usual weather conditions in Latium) bringing a good yield of grain. Misapplication of this practical connection leads to such unsciences as astrology and alchemy and, with the Romans, augury.

The second connection was symbolic. It linked the community not to the natural event but to its emotional content. Whereas the first connection pointed to the future and helped raise crops, the second expressed an immediately present emotion. It soothed spring fever or gave form to fear of thunderstorms.

There are other kinds of connections—a social connection between men and men that results in systems of government; an intimate connection between one man and one other. Today we have one which might be called the physical or legal connection that leads to formulation of scientific laws, not in themselves bound to the present or the future or necessarily to any visible ends. We've also got a monster—the anthropotechnic connection between man and machine. Any one of these connections may of course also have a symbolic counterpart that finds expression in some mode of art.

Well. Although the beginnings of urbanization in eighth-century Latium had severed many people from the soil and commerce had begun to usurp agriculture's economic primacy, although technological advances had made it possible for a part of the group to support the whole and freed another part to exercise talents and interests in occupational specialties not directly related to bodily survival, the traditional ideas enforced a Neolithic cooperate or starve conformity and the interests of the community were generally held then (and for another twelve hundred patriotic years) to be paramount to those of any one member. Although with population growth the body of Roman law had also begun to grow, its straightforwardness cleansing taboo's metaphors from the regulations of human conduct, the traditional ideas locked power in the sanctuaries and jealous persons of the anciently governing, newly merchant priests, who were the absolute repositories of the law, writing, and the calendar.

The eighth-century priestsongs, the Salian hymns, clearly express, for all their now-corruptions, the Neolithic farmers' singleminded survival drive and the general human desire for orientation amid natural chaos. The hymns record some observations of natural facts affecting agriculture. The giving of proper names—metaphors—to these facts, the cyclic March-October ritual context of the hymns, and the hymns' technical devices—rhythm and repetition—make the Salian songs Latin's oldest verbal expressions of the symbolic connection. Of *religio*, which means a binding, a connection. Each proper name embodies communal emotion crystallized, pearllike, around a grain of literal, recurrent fact; and that emotion, become inseparable from the fact, is fact's real *numen* and later its godhead. *Lucesie* and *Curis*, lightning and spear, are not only names for the lightning-fact but for the group's terror in the sound-blasted, brightness-raked darkness of storm. They may be hopes, too, that seeds newly planted be watered, not drowned, by the rains that may come with the lightning. Or may not come at all. *Duonus Cerus* (*Bonus Creator* in classical Latin) is the fact of fertility and also the human passion that responds to spring's foalings and farrowings and urgent green resurrections. *Ianus* is the fact of sun balanced at equinox between the year past and the year-to-be, between the reign of night and the triumph of day. Is sorrow and nostalgia sharing heartroom with excited anticipation. *Consus* is the fact of the stored harvest. Is joy for bellies that bulge with child, not with hunger; is reassurance that famine will not shrink arms, legs, minds. *Mars* is the fact of the coincidence of war's semester with the growing season. Is somber recognition that *media vita in morte sumus*. Is the paradox that man inherits his death at birth but during the years of his dying must keep fueling life and fighting for it. And these names are many other feelings that can perhaps only be sensed in their context of sun's spring warmth on the skin and the sight of green winter wheat slicing the earth and the dance giving body's whole force to the words.

The establishments of the symbolic connection that I read in these words are not primitive in themselves. The primitivity of the Salian rites lies in what happened to them after they were made, in human attempts to treat the symbolic connection as a practical one; with employment of the symbolic connection to influence its generative facts; with subordination of expressed present emotion to possibilities for tangible future results; and with the reduction of metaphoric meaning to literal meaning. It does not seem likely to me that in the moments of the Salian hymns' creation the singers were deliberately *invoking* spirits and making an intentional survival *magic*. (Poetry has a built-in practical effect on people, not things; it changes human perceptions of the world, not the world itself.) The words were chosen rather because they *evoked* emotions through their associations. Of *invocatory* practice, more later.

Archaic thought: the child's mindstyle as Camena

Dark, dark night.
The trees. The river.
One more day;
For so slow goes the day.
Before the end
    the world goes round
        once more.
The world begins the day.
The night has gone.
The day for the end of the world
    once more begins.
Once more begins the sun;
Slow, so slow.
Go on, world, live.
Begin, sweet sun.
Begin, sweet world.
The people live and die.
    People die alive
       alive
         alive.

—Lynette Joass, age 12

The Salian hymns show a childlike quality that has stunning parallels in both the phraseology and import of Lynette Joass's poem. The Roman incantor and the twelve-year-old girl from New Zealand both sing of sun and world and beginnings. In both poems there is a sense of man as phoenix rising again and again out of his own death. This child-quality could not have been superimposed on the hymns as primitivity was superimposed by social use. It must have existed from the moment of first singing. It may have been an impetus to the hymns' use as magic, for children (and poets) are natural magicians. Undomesticated in thought and the application of scientific laws, they make their own laws from what they see and feel and remember, and they use these as-if laws to order their worlds. As the epistemologist Jean Piaget has written:

> We can . . . refer to the striking resemblances between the beginnings of rational thought in the child of from seven to ten and in the Greeks. . . . Are we then to conclude that the archetypes which inspired the beginnings of Greek physics are inherited by the child? In our opinion it is infinitely simpler merely to assume that the same genetic mechanisms which account for the development of the thought of the child of to-day were in action also in the minds of those who, like the pre-Socratics, were just emerging from mythological and pre-logical thought. . . .
>
> To sum up, where there is convergence between the thought of the child and historical representations, it is much easier to explain the latter by the general laws of infantile mentality than by reference to a mysterious heredity. However far back we go in history or pre-history, the child has always preceded the adult, and it can be assumed that the more primitive a society, the more lasting the influence of the child's thought on the individual's development, since such a society is not yet capable of transmitting or forming a scientific culture.
>
> If this is true of thought in general, there is no reason why it should not be true of symbolic thought in particular. . . .[16]

True of symbolic thought. And true therefore of that mode of symbolic thought called poetry. The child mixes metaphor with literal meaning, confounds symbol with thing symbolized.[17] So, as we have seen, do the Salian hymns. The child attributes conscious life to natural phenomena and assigns them motive.[18] So did the Salians when they named the lightning and asked thunder why it rolled on the right. (The idea of thunder on the right as a sign of bad luck is an example of a primitive practical connection.) Up to the attainment of formal thought processes, the child tries to adjust the world to himself.[19] The very early overt use of the Salian rites as magic, not as satisfaction of orientation-need, was a similar attempt to adjust the nonhuman world to the human one. Then, like the child with imaginary friends, the Salian poets gave names to their feelings and in the naming assumed a kind of power over them. And the verb that drives the hymns is a child's (and poet's) verb—*cano*, I sing. It is a verb that takes the direct object, as may the English "dream." People sometimes speak of dreaming something, not dreaming of it, almost as if the act made the objects and events dreamed real and palpable. *Divom templa cante*, the Salians demanded. *The spirit, its holy places—sing them!* As if the singing itself created the spirit and the holy places. And so, in a sense, it really did, for it certainly created the self-contained poetic paraworld of spirit and holy places. The *cano* effect appears deliberately and strikingly in poetry more recent than the Salian hymns. *Arma virumque cano*—I sing arms and the man, wrote Vergil and brought into being the world of the *Aeneid*. Walt Whitman sang himself. And there is Wallace Stevens's woman who

> . . . when she sang, the sea
> Whatever self it had, became the self
> That was her song, for she was maker. Then we,
> As we beheld her striding there alone,
> Knew that there never was a world for her
> Except the one she sang and, singing, made.

> —from "The Idea of Order at Key West"

Having undertaken this inquiry into archaic thought at the level of imagination rather than strictly documentable fact, I come to the inconclusion that the hymns' creators could have been real children. But is something even as slight as an inconclusion warranted by isolated, rotted lines? Is it justified by seeming parallels in the poem of a twentieth-century child? Not at all. It is, however, given a bit of buttressing by late eyewitness testimony about the Salians and their rites. Lucilius,

the Roman satirist, wrote about them in the second century
B.C., and a hundred years later the Greek antiquarian Dionysius
of Halicarnassus described them in his *Roman Antiquities*. If
their Salian facts are to be applied pastward to the hymns'
creators, it must of course first be assumed that the creators
were proto-Salians. No proof supports or contradicts the as-
sumption, and in the void of proof, salianescence seems worth
a brief consideration.

Lucilius described the Salian priests as adolescent boys
with their first small beards (349). According to Dionysius,
some of the prerequisites to membership in either of the two
Salian colleges in first-century B.C. Rome were maleness, bodily
grace; physical adolescence; free, native, noble birth; and exis-
tence (in an age when death often walked in the shadow of
birth) of both a living mother and a living father (II.70.1.4;
71.4). The last prerequisite provided a generation of adults to
stand as living shields between their sons' life-magic and the
possibility of its vitiation by death. Dionysius also compared
the Salians to the Greek Kourētes, a group of youths who per-
formed analogous leaping-singing ceremonies (II.70.3–4). The
comparison is probably accurate and has been extended to other
ancient groups such as the Korybantes of Phrygia.[20] And like
the rites of Kouros and Korybant, the Salian rites may very
possibly have been survivals of tribal initiation rites in which
boy became man. For, the Salian ceremonies occurred promi-
nently in March, the month in which young Romans tradi-
tionally donned the dress of a man and became eligible for the
man's work of soldiering.[21] Thus, it does seem possible that
the hymns' creators, like the priestly performers, could have
been boys whose bodies had begun to take them into physical
maturity. Whose minds remained deep in archaic childhood.

> Help us, household spirits.
> Let not blight and ruin, Mars, hurt more people.
> Be satisfied, fierce Mars: jump the threshold: halt:
>   wet the earth.
> In turn, call on all the seed spirits.

Help us, Mars.
Leap, leap, leap, leap, leap!
—prose approximation of the Arval Chant

It's harder to arrive at inconclusions about the Arval Brothers. We have a fiction: Romulus was the founder of the brotherhood (Aulus Gellius, *Noctium Atticarum*, VII.vii.5–8). And we have facts. They come primarily from remains, dating from A.D. 14 to 241, of the brotherhood's own records, which were engraved on bronze and marble tablets. Our version of the chant is taken from marble engraved in A.D. 218. The brotherhood is said to have performed its ritual at least as late as A.D. 304, in the reign of the emperor Diocletian. But between the brotherhood's historically inaccessible origin and Augustus's politically motivated first-century A.D. revival of its ritual and other native rites that had been overshadowed in late Republican years by foreign cults, there is murk. And supposition on the part of scholars: that the brotherhood originated in the fifth century B.C.;[22] that not Mars as vegetation spirit but Ceres under the name Dea Dia was the *numen* central to the rites.[23] It is likely that the rite was first performed at planting time but was later transferred to the time of ripening or reaping.[24] The chant itself, however, burns in the darkness like a small hot truth. Like the Salian hymns it is indigenous to Italy and very old and magical. Its words say that it first found singing on the tongues of a farming people, and it echoes their green rites of field and grove, even though it came to be closed within the walls of an imperial temple. The five-times repeated final word of the chant—*triumpe!* leap!—clearly establishes its kinship to the Salian hymns and to the Greek dithyramb which—before tragedy took root in it, tragedy being a type of survival poetry, and Pindar gave it great glory—was a springtime song-dance performed with a leaping step.[25] The dithyramb celebrated re-creation through images of birth and was used in the rites that turned boys into men.[26] Arval chant, Salian hymns, and dithyramb—all may have sprung from one common Mediterranean or Indo-

European prototype; the need expressed is more than Mediterranean, it is universal—Lord, keep safe our bodies and our group-soul. Unlike the hymns, however, the chant is directly invocatory and would seem therefore to reflect poetic practices later than those of the hymns, even though legend gives the chant to Romulus and the hymns to his successor Numa. The notable device of the Arval chant is triple iteration of all but the final line, though it cannot be said with any certainty that this repetition existed *ab origine* or was consciously employed. Nor is it known that the Salian hymns did not also use repetition, which is a stock device in primitive and traditional poetry. And in children's stories and rhymes.

One would expect that, like its Salian and Greek counterparts, the Arval chant of greening and survival would have been ritually sung, if not invented, by boys in the springtime of their energy. But the written records make mind's eye see mainly a ceremony of animal sacrifices, feasts, and processions performed by twelve grown men, some of them old. In the Augustan revival eleven brothers were elected for life from notable senatorial families. The twelfth member was the reigning emperor. (The British Museum's bust of Marcus Aurelius, who died in A.D. 180 at the age of fifty-nine, shows him in Arval headdress.) Where is the living armor, then, that protected Arval magic from contamination by death? In the bodies of the brotherhood's four young acolytes, who were both sons of senators and sons of living parents.

Both of these criteria are grounds for inference. First, like the Salian rites, the chant and its ritual performance seem to have been possessed from the beginning by the aristocracy and, more specifically, by priests chosen from that aristocracy. The rites were possessions to which ordinary people had access only through eyes and ears and need for connective symbols. The fiction of royal origins for chant and hymns seems to hold a jot of truth: it could be a way of saying that both rites were the preserve of kings and noblemen. Or, more likely, their sons. For—and this is the second inference—the historically attested existence of the acolytes can be viewed as a late and economic expression of an ancient totality. The Arval brotherhood in its early days was probably composed solely of adolescent boys. And their chant would have followed the Salian pattern from numinous inspiration to use as a sacred magic. Because the Arval rite expressed connections very similar to those of the Salian rites and were once performed at the same time of year, the transfer of the former from planting to harvest time suggests that it was acquired from a source outside Rome (through Roman capture of its practitioners?) at a date later than that of the Salian rites and that it, as the junior ceremony, yielded its place on the religious calendar to the homegrown rites in order to avoid duplication.

Did the survival poets—real boys or men with boys' minds—know they were poets? Did they deliberately set about fashioning hymns and chant? (We may postulate more than one hymnmaker because there are hymns-plural, not necessarily of contemporaneous origin.) For the poets there was surely a first quick pleasure in finding words—not invented but from a traditional stock—that entered a preexisting rhythm like patches of sky suddenly fitting into a jigsaw puzzle. As children or archaically childlike adults, the poets would have been more concerned with the things they sang about than with the manner of singing. As primitive people they most likely believed in an external source of inspiration as the primary fount of their poems, no matter how great the degree of their voluntary collaboration with inspiration, for primitive children and adults alike tend widely (though by no means invariably) to attribute inspiration to a god or ancestral spirit or other form of Muse-power. Individual and group belief in an external Muse-power, in whatever form, may be understood this way: because more than one person—a whole mob, in fact—can share the same numinous experience of the same thing, be it poem-religious service-visit to a haunted house or grove, the experience seems, because of its collective nature, not to be capable of originating in one human body and to be therefore the property of an object or place; it is a simple step from this notion of extrahuman origin to that of holy origin. (This explanation notwithstanding, what poet today can give a completely rational account of the attack of memories and emotions and need that drives him to poem? A sense of *numen* persists. And, if the poet is to make the poem-world in which the laws and logic of the everyday world are often violated, so must persist a large measure of thought that has not been constrained by formal patterning.) Because there was little honor in personal accomplishment or encouragement for it in the early agricultural villages of Latium, any refining of the poem would likely have been done before the poem was presented publicly. If there was refining, it might have occurred through informal joint effort or an arrangement like that in which some Gilbert Islands songs are given public form: they begin with one poet's inspiration and end as creations for which he is deemed responsible but interim have been criticized and directed toward final form by five friends whom the poet has chosen for this task.[27] The Latin poet's name, even if briefly remembered, would be forgotten because it was not likely to have been written down and because his work would have been attributed to the Camenae. The poet, moreover, was not called a poet. The word *poeta* with its implications of deliberate making was not adopted by Latin from the Greek ποιητής until the time of iron poetry. The poet may instead have been called *vates* or prophet, in the biblical sense. Nor was there a profession of poet in preurban Rome, and the young priests were not allowed to grow old in the practice of their singing and dancing.

However many Salian and Arval poets there may have been in however many generations, their movements-tunes-words encoded feelings that were not their sole property but were general to the society. By adopting hymns and chant on the group's behalf, its leaders would have been inspiration's ultimate collaborators.

THE POETRY OF SURVIVAL: ITS ROMAN PRACTICE

Orientation-need, its resolution through rhythmic speech, priestly adoption and containment of such song for social benefit, magical application—these were the beginnings of survival poetry in Rome. And they were also the determinants of bronze practice from the preurban eighth century until the slow decades of change to iron began almost four hundred years later.

Though in these centuries priestly power was increasingly derived from secular sources—control of commerce and the like, life members of the priesthood kept their prehistoric religious authority as conservators of tradition and the vital connections. The Roman year continued to revolve according to an agricultural calendar organized in a time that life was lived close to the bone. And during those centuries the practice of survival poetry remained a wholly sacred matter inextricably associated with the old solemn dance of fat and hungry seasons. While the priests certainly took personal political advantage of their religious authority to imply that *numen* inhabited their secular words and deeds as well as sacred ones, it would have been difficult for them, even in the daylight areas of their minds, to doubt that their religious duties were of divine provenance and that the songs held intrinsically granted truths. In the first place they were blinkered by inherited jobs that required them to preserve tradition, not to add to it, and to repeat what had been told them rather than think for themselves. Most of their songs were neither invented nor put together out of existing materials during their lifetimes but were taught by elder hierarchs who in turn had received them from still an older generation. Most of the songs had no known human origin. The songs' very endurance could have quashed any upstart notion that they rose in a source as impermanent as flesh, especially in flesh that could not, as I've suggested, have been fully cooperative with inspiration. More important, in those days of magic, priesthood carried with it a public obligation that outweighed private allegiances to family and position and was not limited like a Demodocus's responsibility to craft, guild, patron, and belly. The priests sang not to entertain, not for joy or sorrow, but for the material well-being of the people. Attention was not turned to the song of survival itself, nor was the priest-practitioner considered responsible for the words he sang and how he sang them. The pragmatic Romans tested the singer against the goodness of his intent and the song against the *expectation* of perceptible results that it aroused. (Imagine a contemporary criticism that so judges poem and poet. We could then praise Lynette Joass for giving us the expectation of world-beginning and sweet sunrise.) The song was not measured against the results themselves. Magic taken literally is an obvious folly; even archaic minds would have been able to see discrepancies between effects desired and effects achieved. Yet, wheat red with rust and the wine turning to vinegar and the storehouses empty, the Romans continued to practice their magics for reasons that they in their archaic literal-mindedness could not have analyzed: the survival song still represented, in however verbally distorted a way, the primal symbolic connection between man and nature. And, because magic is really a reflection of human yearning, a failure in effect was not synonymous with a failure of desire. Both priests and witnesses would have felt that whatever actually came to happen, they had done what they humanly could, they had fulfilled their obligations.

By the time we meet the Salian and Arval rituals in written history, they have been frozen within the body of traditional material, and in a seemingly curious reversal of original power they appear to have become antievocatory. For, the attention of performer and watcher alike was no longer directed toward feeling and its verbal encapsulation at all but toward the generative facts and magical attempts to influence these facts. The performer danced and sang that the thunder break and roll luckily on the left and the crops be cornucopious and the tribes untribulated by *numina* or one another. New injections of feeling into the performance or an ungradual change in the words, tune, or three-step would have engendered an ominous reaction of unease by recentering attention in the ritual itself. This unease would be externalized and understood as the displeasure of the *numen* the ritual was thought to invoke. This effect may well be the reason that a Roman religious ritual malperformed in the slightest detail was a religious ritual wholly repeated until it soothed the people (not, as they thought, the spirits) with its antique perfection. And certainly it is the reason that, as the Roman orator Quintilian wrote in the first century A.D., ". . . though . . . the *carmina* of the Salians are hardly intelligible to their own priests, religion forbids that they be altered, and they must be used as wholly sacred things" (*Institutio Oratoria*, I.vi.40). Even as nonsense the performed hymns were songs that comforted because they aroused no feelings of disorientation. (Think of Americans listening to a Latin mass; they do not understand the words but in the context of liturgical calendar-church-chime-chalice the import of the words is felt and an omission would be noted.) Survival rites and songs lasted out the long centuries because they continued, though less and less directly, to serve as necessary, formal symbolic expressions of human feeling. And through the centuries of bronze illiteracy they provided the people with sensible documents of an historical continuum. They were chords linking the legendary past to the here-now moment, and their reality was audible proof that the past was real, too.

But what if, in those dark centuries, a Roman wanted to sing a new arrangement of old sacred words? Two lives could have depended on the singer's expectations: the life of the song in the canon of spells and the life of the singer himself. Words were moons, each with a dayside and a nightside, not seen but there nonetheless. Accepted meaning was joined to its opposite. Words thought to be holy with a power for public good could also serve to create expectations of blight or an untimely sepulcher. The law, therefore, taped the would-be singer's mouth and obviated most possibilities for innovation in survival poetry. As a primary consequence many of the survival songs legally permitted voice were those sanctioned by a history of imputed benefaction (not bene*diction*) or by fears of omission. The consequence most painful now is that bronze Latin's inevitably time-reduced chances for transcription and transmittal down the millennia were long ago made even slimmer by statute. In 451 and 450 B.C. the Romans were given the first public codification of the laws that had been—tales of Kafka—the secret, sacred knowledge of the patrician priests. Fragments of these laws, called The Twelve Tables because they were first engraved on that number of bronze tablets, have luckily been preserved in the writings of later authors. Some of the laws deal directly and grimly with poetic creation. Two indict him "who shall have chanted an evil charm" (VIII.1b) and "who has chanted away the fruits of the land" and "coaxed away another man's grain" (VIII.8a–b). Another prohibits sticking verbal voodoo pins into real people: "If anyone has chanted or made a charm that slandered another man or made him infamous, he shall be beaten to death with cudgels" (VIII.1a).[28] Versefinding for the public good might be reputable. Verse*making*, the expression of private interest, was a capital crime. Yet, in Rome there were other kinds of poetic endeavor that did not carry threats of punishment and death.

THE POETRY OF CELEBRATION

A Camena-stung Roman seems to have been allowed some freedom in versemaking. Unfortunately, there is little bronze poetry of celebration left. Bronze practice must be inferred from later references to its existence and from applying pastward what is known about iron and classical practices. Celebration seems to have had several bronze forms. A poet could compose dirges and eulogies to honor the dead and propitiate their spirits. He could make epitaphs. And he could sing a song in praise of a victorious general. The historian Livy (59 B.C.–A.D. 17) wrote of an occasion in 458 B.C.:

At Rome the senate, called into session by Quintus Fabius, prefect of the city, ordered Quinctius to enter the city in triumph with his troops. Led before his chariot were the enemy's generals; the military standards were carried ahead, and the soldiers, burdened with loot, followed. It is said that feasts were set in front of every house, and the feasting soldiers followed the chariot like revelers with triumphal song and the usual jokes.

—III.xxix.4–5

Here Livy may have been using his knowledge of the usual mechanics of a triumph to give life to a shadowy occasion; written records pertaining to 458 B.C. were mostly destroyed by the Gauls sixty years later. But it hardly matters whether there really was a triumphal song, or even a triumph, in 458 because, victory over an enemy being a universal occasion for explosive joy, there are so many examples of ancient triumphal song that one finds it difficult to doubt their existence in belligerent bronze Rome.

Any celebration poetry would have been created voluntarily for the particular occasion to relate the exemplary exploits of the man of the hour, were he alive or newly dead. In celebratory commemoration of historical personages lies one source of the iron epic. There is no evidence now that Rome possessed a bronze epic of even mini-Homeric dimensions or that it had a fund of heroic ballads like those Macauley postulated by writing *Lays of Ancient Rome*, but it's hard to agree with the from-Missouri people who deny absolutely the possibility of a modest bronze Latin balladry. The women who sang the preserved lullaby to their children surely told them stories, and the easiest way to remember and retell a story without benefit of print is adding dashes of formular language and jingle that begin to separate it technically, if minimally, from prose. What stories more likely than those of old Uncle Remus and Romulus and the current hero? Neither legendary figures nor historic personages sprang full-grown into their epic incarnations from the brows of the professional iron poets.

The surviving few verses of bronze celebration are third- and second-century B.C. epitaphs written in saturnians. They are superficially boastful, listing offices held and lands vanquished. But the prime idea behind their composition seems to have been *pietas*, that Roman supervirtue that provided a theme for much postbronze poetry and prose. Honors and accomplishments listed in metric précis the ways in which the dead man had served *pietas*. The word means, most simply, a filial devotion to family and state and a reverence for ancestral values. *Pietas* is defined in this sense by an iron elegy in epitaph of Gnaeus Cornelius Scipio Hispanus. It is Greek-metered and dated about 135 B.C., but it is thoroughly bronze in language and sentiment.

> Virtutes generis mieis moribus accumulavi,
>   progenium genui, facta patris petiei.
> Maiorum optenui laudem, ut sibei me esse creatum
>   laetentur; stirpem nobilitavit honor.[29]

> By my conduct I have heaped virtues on my family;
>   I fathered children; I sought to match my father's deeds.
> I have kept intact the praise of my ancestors so that my cre-
>   ation from them
>   makes them rejoice; my honors have given my stock fame.

Pietas is also a religious piety, not toward *numina* or supernatural beings, but toward the attributes and circumstances and human values they represent, be it Mens-Wisdom or Volutina-Way in which hull curls around seed. *Pietas* stiffened Roman backbones with a moral code not supplied by pandemonism and later pantheism. The purpose of personal—not group—survival was inherent in obedience to *pietas*: as my father was, so am I, and so must my sons—fortune willing— be. Where survival poetry—a poetry of the ritual act—was used with unwitting psychology to channel group emotions and as intentional magic to keep people alive and fed, the poetry of celebration—a poetry of the pious and heroic act— was very early used to strengthen traditional patterns of conscious daily thought and behavior.

Though the bronze epitaph-makers and composers of triumphal song certainly exercised poetic volition, their verses were probably not accepted as whole, autonomous worlds of poetic evocation. The poems would have been acclaimed or damned for their explicit surface sentiments. For their morality.

What if someone wanted to sing for the hell of it? Roman practice had its antidotes to serious magic and stern morality. The earliest known of is Fescennine verse. The poet Horace (65–8 B.C.) tells how it began and what it became:

> When, harvest stored and the glad time at hand, our farming forefathers, strong men of small chance for laughter, sought in the company of sons and faithful wives, to lighten their bodies as well as their souls . . . they would appease Earth's spirit with a pig, the Awe that dwells in the dark woods with milk, and every human Power of Procreation . . . with flowers and wine. In this custom arose the Fescennine license that poured out rough insults in alternating verses, and this freedom, allowed in each recurring year, was exercised amiably until the jokes, grown savage, turned freedom into a public madness and with impunity menaced even honest homes.
>
> —*Epistles*, II.i.139–150

This account reads true. The prototypical poetry of possibility seems to have been the spoken, nonaristocratic concomitant to a sacred ceremony, an agricultural rite or perhaps a marriage. It probably originated in the verbal and physical exaggerations of human sexuality that many primitive people use as magics for animal and vegetable fertility. Neither invocative nor evocative but *pro*vocative, it was in any event a steamvalve for country people wound tight with the seriousness and hard work of staying alive. Later, such body-lightening was dissociated from soul-lightening activities, and it became a secular form of emotional eruption. The fact that "the Fescennine license . . . poured out rough insults in alternating verses" suggests an analogy in the contests in sung insults or braggadocio that are enjoyed by many primitive people and theatergoers: I can do anything better than you can.

Horace continues his account:

People bitten by a blood-drawing tooth suffered anguish;
worry about the general state of affairs rose even in those
who were unscathed. And finally a law with a penalty
was passed to forbid that anyone be described in an evil
song. Men changed their ways and dread of drubbing led
them again to wholesome, agreeable speech.

—the same, 150–155

Here Horace plays a false note; the last sentence rings like a
cracked bell. Men did not change their ways. However scurri-
lous, earthy, frank, anatomically descriptive, magicomalicious,
and mordant the Fescennines were, they also commanded
such popularity that The Twelve Tables' anti-infamy clause,
to which Horace refers, was unable to suppress the genre.

What were Fescennines like? No bronze examples survive.
But later authors write to the rescue. Catullus wrote a wedding
poem (61.126–127) that mentions "Fescennine joking" sung
as a prenuptial shivaree as the bride was led to the bride-
groom's house. And postclassical Latin biographers have left
late examples of the type. In these, however neatly Greek the
meters, the genre comes alive. Suetonius (b. A.D. 69?) re-
corded many pop-verses in his tell-all Lives of the Twelve
Caesars. One such ditty is supposed to have been sung by the
soldiers following the chariot of General Julius Caesar at his
Gallic triumph and enjoying their ancient privilege to make
the "usual jokes" mentioned by Livy:

Urbani, servate uxores: moechum calvom adducimus.
Aurum in Gallia effutuisti, hic sumpsisti mutuum.

—Divus Iulius, 51

Citizens, watch your wives: we bring you a hairless adulterer.
He's spent all the fucking in Gaul; here he's taken out loans.

And much later, in a Life of the Deified Aurelian (emperor from
A.D. 270–275) attributed to Flavius Vopiscus (fl. early 4th cen-
tury A.D.), there are embedded two triumphal soldiers' hollers:

Mille mille mille decollavimus.
unus homo mille decollavimus.
mille bibat quisquis mille occidit.
tantum vino nemo habet quantum fudit sanguinis.

—Divus Aurelianus, VI.5

Mille Sarmatas mille Francos semel et semel occidimus,
mille Persas quaerimus.

—the same, VII.2

We've cut off a thousand thousand thousand heads.
One man has cut off a thousand heads.
He'd drink by the thousand who killed by the thousand—
no one has enough wine to match the blood that has spilled.

A thousand Sarmatians, a thousand Franks—again and again
  we've killed them.
Now we look for a thousand Persians.

Mille mille mille murder sits on the soldiers' tongues like the
dry taste of a thousand hangovers and nothing but more blood
spurting from decapitated bodies will sweeten the desert. This
song and the victorious circumstance of its hollering bear, but
for the gender of the singers, a similarity to those mentioned in
I Samuel 18:6–7:

> And it came to pass as they came, when David was re-
> turned from the slaughter of the Philistine, that the women
> came out of all cities of Israel, singing and dancing, to meet
> king Saul, with tabrets, with joy, and with instruments of
> musick.
> And the women answered one another as they played,
> and said, Saul hath slain his thousands, and David his ten
> thousands.

There is a Fescennine sort of insult in the women's song. Saul's
victory is acclaimed but rendered insignificant by comparison

to David's achievements: "And Saul was very wroth, and the saying displeased him. . . ."

In spite of their longevity as a type, in spite of their obviously voluntary creation, Fescennine verses as such never gave their name to a distinct literary genre. Topical, given life by a moment or a human peculiarity only to die when the moment or the singer or the sung-at died, they stayed on the needle tongues of a largely alphabetless people. Their contribution to literary poetry was their tenor. Savageness like theirs appears in Lucilius's iron ridiculing of misers and gluttons and procuresses and in Catullus's classical, exquisitely vicious verses on topics such as fellatio (80).

The bronze poetry of possibility that did enter literature was satire. Its origins are hazy. It seems to have been a form indigenous to Italy, a preliterate folk entertainment, perhaps of a nonprofessional, marginally Commedia dell'Arte nature—stock characters, stock situations, stock business, that traded on improvised and witty opinions but did not have the Fescennines's blood-drawing teeth. The Latin word *satura* means mixture or miscellany, and, applied adjectivally to the word *lanx*, platter, signifies a sort of smorgasbord. This application suggests a connection with harvest celebrations and an ancestral form in common with the Fescennines. Again, alas, no early examples.

THE CHANGE FROM BRONZE TO IRON
The Fifth Century to 240 B.C.

Wherever we find a quickening of the human spirit we are perhaps justified in tracing it back to a situation in which the individual has been released, if but for a short time, from the dominance of the group—its observations, formulas, and ideas.

—Eric Hoffer, *The Ordeal of Change*

The descriptions of Fescennine verses and soldiers' jokes tell nothing of how Rome's poetry of possibility reached the page. Nor do celebration's potential for guiding daily life and survival's constant emotional comfort tell how they too were transmuted into iron. By the end of the fifth century B.C. all three varieties had been established, but they were then merely substance which might—or might not—inform a future, literate poetry. None existed as an art in its own right. Each was instead linked umbilically with the economic, political, or re-creational functions of early religion. Before song could be at all understood as a self-justifying pursuit, it had somehow to cease being reiteration and recombination of ideas from a mossy stockpile. Before the singer could be transformed into a maker, a professional poet, he had to become able to think publicly of himself as an individual not limited by his society's categorical definition of Man.

Iron poetry was a slow miracle. Its apparently sudden appearance in the form of Livius's plays was not, however, a clean break with past practices but a culmination, a surfacing of fires that had eaten away at tradition's innards for a good two hundred and fifty years. The sparks of poetic change were struck by the collision of real conditions, inside and outside Rome's walls, with fossilized beliefs.

Rome's extramural activities during these centuries are well known. In a lurching war dance of treaty-making and treaty-breaking, retreat, hesitation and advance, it battled for self-preservation. At the beginning of the fifth century the culturally alien Etruscan kings were expelled and Rome became a republic. A hundred years later the still regionally threatening Etruscans were defeated at Veii in the battle that decisively flung them toward history's midden, though in downspin they remained troublesome for another century. By 338 Rome had achieved hegemony, O famous schoolbook word, over the other Latin tribes in Latium and was reaching unsteadily northward toward Italy's knobbly Alpine knees, east into the Apulian dewclaw, south into the Greek-dominated bootheel and toe. In 266, with the establishment of control over the entrance to the Adriatic Sea, Rome stood supreme in Italy. Two years later the Romans engaged their first extracaligular enemy, the Carthaginians, in the First Punic War. When a peace was concluded in 241, Rome had gained its first provincial foothold and, defensively predacious as ever, stalked forth into the world. Throughout this period conquests by sword were consolidated with flesh and stones. Rome built a web of military roads and placed colonies like cultural egg sacs in foreign parts. As tribes and towns were encompassed, long-standing but sporadic and war- or trade-filtered contacts with other Mediterranean peoples became direct and permanent, especially in the case of the Greeks. And the military roads, speeding outward communication and deployment of troops, also speeded an inbound traffic in foreign inventions, ideas, goods, and gods. And men. Livius Andronicus was one of the Tarentine Greeks brought as slaves to Rome in 272.

The effects of territorial expansion stormed Roman parochialism, and at the same time the pressures of urbanization were destroying the old social unity based on survival-mandated obedience to the rhythms of sun and soil. The life pattern evolved by herdsmen and farmers to feed their separate bodies and save the group's rural soul had become in many respects a lifethreat to the landless, voteless, disoriented masses—lawless because they did not know the law—who spent their years in the sunless alleys of a city tugged by the rhythms of commerce and war. The threat lay in tradition's perpetuation of attitudes irrelevant to change, its inelasticity, its intolerance of diversity, its inability to meet the city's growing appetite for specialized services other than those of priests, and its absolute failure to support and comfort the independent farmers whose small suburban landholdings were worked out to a point of failing to provide either a livelihood or a meaning for living. One may see soil depletion as a contributing factor to the famed Roman belligerence; it was necessary for Rome to practice predatory economics, to expand and conquer in order to provide the people under its jurisdiction with food. Where political power in the strictly rural villages of early Latium depended, as it often does today in Southern Italy, on religion-hedged control of local food production and distribution, political power in the new pluralistic Rome depended on developing symbiotic secular relationships between specialist and specialist, class and class, indigenous culture and outlandish accretion. From the time of the expulsion of the Etruscan kings, the city was the focus of a protracted, often bloody conflict between the have-nots and the patricians who had long ruled by ordination of the traditional mindset. The struggle calls to mind a batch of current catchphrases—civil rights, social justice, war on poverty, identity crises, population explosion, politics of confrontation. And it held all the polarizing fears and suspicions and prejudices that these words hold today. The ostensible issue to be resolved was temporal power. The real issue was the need on both sides for a reintegrating set of social checks and balances.

Laws surviving from the Republic's first two centuries now document the adjustments in the Roman lifestyle. The adjustments did not constitute a revolution pervading all levels of society; free noncitizens, slaves, and strangers were largely unaffected. Those most affected were the two anciently established orders—the patricians and the plebeians, who were originally a group of free, Latin people under patrician protection. From the 450 B.C. hierarchic publication of The Twelve Tables to the carnage-inspired passage of the Hortensian Laws in 286, the plebeians slowly cracked the patricians' power monopoly and gained theoretical, if not always practicable, equality in many matters. Religious equality: the plebeians forced public revelations of holy knowledge and thus opened a decisive split between sacred matters and secular ones. They obtained admission to some sacred colleges that had been key means of preserving the patricians' old-boy network. Political equality: they won the right for all male Roman citizens, freed as well as freeborn, to seek elective offices. Economic equality: no plebeian was to be enslaved for debt. Social equality: marriages between members of the two orders became lawful.

One man sums up the tensions between discipline and freedom. He was Appius Claudius Caecus, patrician, censor in 312, consul in 296, general, adaptive genius, builder of an aqueduct and the Appian Way, and part-time writer of sententious verse. Like a Janus swung between personal interest and imposed necessity, he was a backward-looking conservative who would deny change and guard hoary, repressive privileges by keeping plebeians out of the sacred colleges and the consulship and, *simul*, he was a futuregazing reformer who encouraged change by giving the vote to freedmen and delivering an old religious rite reserved for patricians into the public custody of slaves. Two of his lines have outlasted him. One, an indirect quotation, attests to an alteration in the Roman mindstyle: *Appius ait fabrum esse suae quemque fortunae.*[30] On its way out the old groupthink of agricultural tradition. Beginning to take its place, the once subversive notion that "Each man is the maker of his own fortune."

And what had foreign adventures and domestic bloodbaths to do with the making of poetry? The change from bronze to iron? By the time of Appius Claudius Greece's classic literature had long been available for the taking. It had arrived by land and sea with the traders and diplomatic envoys; it had come up the military pikes with the slave coffles and wagonloads of loot. But Greek techniques had stayed in Greek hands. Here's what happened to push the Roman singers into poetic adolescence and picking up the tools of men.

As warfare receded from home fields and Rome gained people and land and a dwindling percentage of the population was needed to provide the essential life services of food production and defense, many people found themselves with time on their hands. Though Republican Romans were generally inclined to think that evil made work for idle minds, leisure gave them spare hours to act in causes other than that of bodily necessity. There was time for the unenfranchised to rage at injustice and mount a revolution; there was time for Appius Claudius to contemplate friendship and make a saturnian verse about it, *Amicum cum vides, obliviscere miserias*[31]—When you see a friend, forget your troubles. Then, as Rome founded colonies and began in 286 to extend full citizenship, including the franchise, to some colonists, Latin as a first language spread beyond the confines of Latium, and the potential audience for Latin poetry was enlarged, as was the pool of possible verse-makers. The alphabet was made widely accessible. Domestic revolution unlocked the temples where the written chronicles, inventories, and oracles were kept; war brought writing home as part of the plunder. Also, as the exigencies of trade and territorial and military administration created an open-ended demand for clerks and bookkeepers to staff burgeoning bureaucracies, literacy became a secular necessity. Though the opportunity to become lettered was hardly extended wholesale to the lower classes and the ability to read and write continued to be a mark of status, literacy spread because it was a far better way of storing, retrieving, and disseminating information than reliance on human memory banks. And some illiterate Romans must have found themselves embarrassed by possession of educated slaves: if a slave can read and write, then so can I. With the secularization of writing, poetry too was liberated from the temples and redirected. It was for the first time in Rome separated from the other performed arts by being given a medium of transmission that music and dance could not share. It did continue, however, to find performance in drama—the mode of possibility in comedy, that of survival in tragedy, until literate drama was doomed by the loss of an educated audience in the second century B.C. More important, as cultural diversity presented alternatives to the old groupways in every aspect of life from making a living to selecting religious practices, human aspirations found new reaches. Many Romans were obliged, as Appius pointed out, to make an increasing number of personal decisions affecting their own finite fortunes, and aspiration came to be limited by individual gumption, talent, and accomplishment rather than birth as a patrician, plebeian, or slave. The rise of the individual in fourth- and third-century Rome was surely also encouraged from without by the slow accumulation of victories and by the successes of absorption that could calm old fears of human differences and weaken the old resistance to change and boost self-confidence. Some of the political effects of the new sense of selfpower in a world fashioned of choices have been mentioned. In poetry that sense led to the epiphany of one man's distinctive wordchoices—style. "Judgment, a test . . . what word to use and where to place it," wrote Lucilius (417–418). And, most important to poetry as a written act of volition was its partial takeover by the state. With the disintegration of agriculture-based tradition, new means for ensuring social cohesion had to be found. The leaders of the Republic seized upon poetry as a force for healing the old traumas of change and preventing new ones. With the sudden thrust of Rome into the world, a noble background was needed to cleanse it of barbarism and to account for its power. The leaders turned to the supposed lessons of history for an ethos and to poetry for the texts. They turned to the poets as advocates without understanding that poets were evocates instead.

IRON

240–169 B.C.: Armed with two alphabets, Latin and Greek, the celebrators make history.

Audire est operae pretium procedere recte
qui rem Romanum Latiumque augescere vultis.

Listen and your wage shall be your wish come true:
Rome prospering and Latium growing greater still.

—Ennius, *Annales*, 471–472

In the fires of change, in the catalyzing presence of state need, bronze was transmuted into iron. By the mid-third century B.C. the state began to allow translation and adaptation of tragedy on the grounds that it could edify. (Greek-based comedy was tolerated as an entertainment and censored.) And it began to encourage the production of a secular poetry to be used in teaching, as moral preachments, as propaganda, all for the sake of fostering the desirable national unity. Through sharing educational experiences in a common tongue, men would come to share ideals of thought and action, and they would find a common pride in present leadership as well as in a fiercely glorious, if legendary, past.

The situation was made to order for the celebrators. The survivalists naturally continued to sing the old magical songs and were allowed to make new ones, especially in the form of tragedy. The saturnian meter endured as a kind of stately relic for nonliterary use in triumphal and dedicatory inscriptions. Livy records our first example of a nonlegendary poet's name attached to sacred song and says that in 207 Livius Andronicus made a hymn on priestly request (XXVII.37). It was sung by twenty-seven girls to invoke Juno's intercession against the evils promised by several distressing omens. This hymn is lost. Nor do any other iron hymns now exist, though one can imagine a booming post-Livian hymn business as religious festivals multiplied and omens kept looming. During the latter half of the Republic foreign cults were introduced by the dozens and lapsed native rituals were occasionally revived to serve as placebo, let-'em-eat-cake holidays for a disgruntled proletariat. But the kind of orientation-need—the need for men to make connections between themselves and natural forces or gods representing those forces—that engendered survival songs was overshadowed by the newer need for men to find new sets of connections between themselves. The poetry of possibility was to lurk on the fringes of legality for another hundred years, until the second century's halfway mark, when still other desperate needs for belief to catch up to reality would make the poets bold enough to flout the law consistently and at the same time would loosen the law's grip on its poet-beating cudgels. But the celebrators, blessed by the ascription of social utility to their constructs, responded to state prodding as if to the Camenae themselves. Finding no homegrown conventions large enough for their ideas of history and fate and morality, they began to step bravely toward Greek techniques. And tumbled into a lion's den of critics—literary and political.

The making of iron celebrations, narrative or dramatic in

the form of historical plays, was hedged by criteria that may seem distorted but were anciently pervasive and are not at all uncommon today, especially where state sponsorship or control is involved. The poet Horace described the celebrator's responsibilities:

> Though he is lazy and inept on the battlefield, he's useful to the state if you grant that by little things great ones are served. The poet forms the tender, stuttering speech of a child; he turns the ear from obscene words, and soon he shapes emotion with friendly precepts. He is the corrector of harshness and envy and anger, he rightly relates deeds, he instructs the rising times with notable examples, he consoles the weak and the sick.
>
> —*Epistles*, II.i.125–131

Speaking of playwriting in his own golden day Horace expressed a view that applies as well to iron celebration: "Either to be useful or to delight is what the poets wish, or to say something at once pleasant and suitable to life" (*Ars Poetica*, 333–334). He also wrote that pleasant and suitable and useful poetry "though of no grace, without authority or art, pleases the people much more and captivates them better than does euphonious nonsense or verse empty of ideas" (the same, 320–322). In other words, an artistic failure containing the "right" ideas was more to be desired than an artistic success containing subversive ones. The iron celebrator's broad choice would seem to have rested between writing to edify or not writing at all, for the state's delight rose not in well-made art but in the positive efficacy of the poem's teaching. And the poem's moral and factual burdens rather than its total construction determined its value to the critics. It seems fair to suggest that at least part of the poets' ardor for Greek literature sprang from being able to shrug off inutile, unsuitable unpleasantnesses onto Greek originals.

There was another circumscription to the writing of poetry in the general suspicion, to which poets themselves were mune, that poetry—unless guided carefully by maker or state—would deal willy-nilly not only in anathematic ideas but in outright falsehoods, those lies on the Muses' tongues of which Hesiod was wary. This attitude reflects a not unusual institutional or group distrust of independent thought. The orator Quintilian (b. A.D. 35?) called the storylines of poems *fabulae* —a word equivalent to Sextus Empiricus's *mythos*—and declared that "*fabulae* such as those in tragedies and poems are not only not the truth but remote from the semblance of truth" (work cited, II.iv.2; V.xi.17). And a century earlier Cicero had asked, "What is so contrived as verses, stagesets, plays?" (*de Oratore*, II.46.193). In these hardly uncommon views the poem was made and made *up*, a total fiction. Such prejudice is understandable when it is seen to stem from a belief that the poem should deal in verity rather than verisimilitude (or, as Mrs. Langer put it, "virtual life"). That the poem should tell a truth rather than make one. Aristotle had recognized long before Latin poetry's iron age that a poem can deal with probable impossibilities—a self-contained logic—rather than documentable facts (work cited, 1460a.26–27; 1461b.11–12). And he had asked that each poem be judged uniquely for the appropriateness of the delight—orientation!—it actually did originate in itself (the same, 1453b.11–12; 1462b.13–14; and other places) rather than for its fulfillment of a listener's expectations. But these thoughts—valid ones, I believe—failed to filter Romeward through the niggling pedantry of Hellenistic scholarship and criticism. There seems to have been no notion in Rome that a reader or hearer should come to a poem as to the shore of an unknown country.

Given iron working conditions that defined poetry both by its imputed utility and by its adherence to rigid *sine qua non* laws of prosody, the poet desiring acceptance faced the trap of committing himself, not always unintentionally, to the truth of the strictures of his craft rather than to the truth of his poetic impulses. He was certainly encouraged to follow the former course by a conviction on the part of many Romans (and Greeks—Plato for one) that poetry was not a pursuit for normal, responsible men and that poets were quite literally mad, obeying voices nobody else could hear, following visions nobody else could see, and telling the most seductive lies. Cato the Elder (234–149 B.C.), that iron minder of everyone's manners, voiced the disapproval and uneasiness of a conservative multitude in his own longing recollection of the good old lost days when "There was no honor in the art of poetry: if a man studied it or applied himself to conviviality, he was called a vagabond" (quoted by Aulus Gellius, work cited, XI.ii.5). Cato might have been writing of medieval Goliards or our peripatetic, beat nineteen-fifties. And there were those men who, in the eyes of Rome's establishment, incarnated its fears of madness by committing themselves to the appearance of being "poets." From his security within that establishment, Horace, sounding like a Nostradamus for the hairy, tripping sixties or a bearer of ironic beatitudes, described the Roman scene:

> Because Democritus thinks that talent [manic inspiration, that is] is a luckier thing than miserable art [applied techniques] and excludes sane poets from Helicon, a good many young men take no care to trim their nails or beards but take refuge in secret places and avoid the baths. For surely the rewards and name of poet will shower down on him who never yields his head to the barber. . . .
>
> —*Ars Poetica*, 295–301

Stay put, stay sober, shear, shave, and bathe. Or perish. How many did?

Of those iron celebrators who did not perish, there are two—Naevius (270?–201?) and Ennius (239–169)—who show that obedience to the laws of craft and demands of state could be compatible with preserving integrity of impulse. Between them they put paid to the canard that Latin poets were the diminished echoes of Greece's great voices. Granted, the iron period was an age of adaptation, but adaptation, as distinct from translations and wholesale trading in Homeric similes and plodding along in Greekish feet, should not be confused with lack of originality. Adaptation conferred technical benefits upon the poem and personal ones upon the poet. It could be a state-deceiving disguise for independent thought, a compliment to an unbeatable line or device, and a boast that the imitator could write at least as well as his model. Although criticism did fix boundaries on practice and tried to set them for ideas, it is accurate to see the iron age of Latin poetry as one of exploration, of discovering new reaches for language and communication as extreme as the antithetical abandonment of strict forms and metrics was to the early twentieth century. As exciting as escaping the confines of the page is now to the concretists who build poems or fly them on kites and to the poets on the reading circuits who have rediscovered both listeners and the voice as an instrument. The fragments of iron celebration show the first literary uses of that typically Roman, not Greek-derived, device—alliteration; alliteration seems to have been appropriated from sacred formulae in which it had a primitive magical significance.[32] The fragments show the fun of inventing outrageous compound words and the frustrations of squashing Latin into hexameters. They show poetic purpose crumbling before the temptation to flaunt learning, and that purpose then restored by the use of allusions and untranslated quotations in a fashion that predicts Pound. The ultimately successful adaptations of Greek techniques and ideas also represented a success in liberal political thinking, a rejection of the Catos. There were failures of course, and they were grandiose. And important because they illustrate a constant push toward the limits of semantic and human capabilities. The successes resound still in the graecolatinity of many languages. The iron celebrators began the stabilization of Latin grammar and orthography. Their inventions and borrowings exploded Latin's vocabulary. And in marking these courses for both future Latin poems and prose, the iron lines prove Emerson's aphorism that "language is fossil poetry." At worst, the celebrations have reached us as fossils, grit settling into the mold left by the decay of living substance. At their best, they can re-create—

here, now—a virtual experience of Rome's horrors and its splendors. In their major resources—history and legend—the celebrators were fortunate, for history and legend record unpleasantnesses and defeats as well as triumphs. In manipulating what even the critics believed to be facts, the poets found a loophole in critical limits. And created a "virtual history," a set of group memories based not on actual events but on poetic apprehension of those events. The aim of the state was stability, but in letting the poets loose, the state opened the gate to new perceptions of the world. Far from stopping change, the poets speeded it. All they froze was the past. Between them Ennius and Naevius so solidly froze it in paraworlds that today's schoolbook histories of Rome reflect virtual history almost as often as actual history, despite the diligence of the scholars.

Naevius, Roman citizen, member of an old plebeian family, was Latin poetry's first known major celebrator. Livius Andronicus, however much he has come to mark the instant of bronze Latin's failure, cannot be granted that title. For, he took the literature he was born to—the narratives and dramas and godsongs of Greek experience—and rephrased them in alien words. The remains of his work—we have only minifragments of the awkwardly saturnian, *Odyssey* and a few Greek-metered dramatic bits—demonstrate merely that he was educated, not that he had literary talent. Consider him a floodgate, lifted at the state's behest, that helped speed the tide of Greek ideas and let the Roman poets rise. Naevius was the first true *princeps* of literary celebration, for he made it his business to give virtual life to the dark inward glories of Roman experience in the words and rhythms that had always been part of that experience.

The historians of Latin literature have generally given Naevius short shrift and acclaimed his successor-in-celebration Ennius as the "father of Latin poetry." There's some reason for this dismissal of Naevian achievement. The fragments of his work show it to have been technically primitive in comparison to the poetry that came immediately after. Though he used

Greek meters for adaptations of Greek comedies and tragedies, he looked suspiciously on Greek gifts when it came to making verses on Roman subjects, and he chose the old holy stifflegged saturnians as the rhythm appropriate to his epic *Song of the Punic War*. (THUDding BUMPing and STOMPing/METrics are opPRESsive. Try listening to that, with exceeding minor variations, for a thousand lines.) But while the meter does indeed detract from the poem's force, it cannot hide Naevius's profoundly original contributions to the poetry of celebration. *The Song of the Punic War* marks the first now-existing appearance in Western poetry of an important protagonist. No Achilles, Odysseus, or Jason, no philosophic idea drove that poem. The force behind the action is not a hero but an heroic concept—*romanitas*, a summing of events and people and virtues that equaled a proud sense of Roman destiny and gave the Romans a new reason for being. *The Song of the Punic War* tells a big chapter in the wrath of Rome. A Rome that had little sense of history until its martial emergence into the world compelled it to find one. A second Naevian innovation is the use of contemporary facts as a skeleton for epic. The poem begins in legend—the flight of Aeneas from burning Troy and his arrival in Italy, the birth of Romulus and his founding of Rome, King Numa's institution of the sacred laws. But its bulk is a narrative based on a real war, which began in Naevius's childhood and ended when he was about thirty years old. Whatever he could not remember, he could gather from documents or the yarns of veterans. Naevius's break with past practice was also signified by his poem's bold expression of the new mindstyle. It is the first Latin poem that presents a Roman sense of time as an onflowing river rather than a circular movement whose recurring stations are indicated, like numbers on a clockface, by yearly repeated, unchanging rituals.

Romanitas, narratives of verifiable events, epic presentation of incontrovertibly real heroes, a view of time as a linear progression—for the use of these in Latin epic, Ennius is surely somewhat indebted to Naevius. The debt is acknowledged by an omission. With reason Ennius considered himself the first

Roman poet truly aware of his creative role, his duty to answer inspiration with wits as well as tongue and to apply strict rules of craft. He scornfully consigned all who had gone before him to the unenlightened realms of Fauns and soothsayers. Yet, on the grounds that "others have written verses on the subject" (*Annales*, 231–232), he excused the brief treatment of the First Punic War in his own epic *Annals*, a poem that traced Rome's fortunes from the fall of Troy through at least the Second Punic War. Such summary handling of an epic-worthy subject seems odd; one would not expect Ennius to refrain from a virtuoso performance. But when Ennian scorn is seen to be aimed at Naevius's primitive craftsmanship and supposed reliance on inspiration rather than "miserable art," Ennian brevity becomes a tacit gesture of respect to the elder poet's originality and his very real resolutions of orientation-need.

With Ennius Latin poetry was set firmly on the course of volition. And his clear right to be called the father of Latin poetry stems from many firsts. He really was, as he boasted with forgivable arrogance, the first Roman to abandon oral, preliterate conventions and "climb the rocks of the Muses" (the same, 233). He was the first deliberately "devoted to the study of style" (the same, 234) and the first to tame Latin with hexameters and call his work *poemata* rather than *carmina*, made things rather than songs. He was the first to apply Muse-techniques consistently and often successfully to everything he wrote during a prolific lifetime. Aside from the fragments of his masterwork, the *Annals*, we have chunks and shreds of adapted Greek tragedies and comedies, a poem in praise of General Scipio Africanus, several satires, a translation—probably in prose—of Greek myths, metric translations of both didactic poems and some verses on pleasant things to eat, and two original plays on historical Roman subjects.

There seem to be several reasons for Ennius's lifelong purveyance of Greek techniques and thought, even to the extent of losing his first Roman patron, Cato the Elder whose conservatism made him think of Greek ideas as concealments for all manner of Greek evils: ". . . when those people [the Greeks] give their letters, they corrupt everything" (Cato quoted by Pliny, *Natural History*, 29.14). The most obvious reason is that Greek ideas must have been ineradicably impressed on Ennius in childhood, for he was born in a Roman colony in Calabria, not far from Greek Brundisium (modern Brindisi), and lived there till military service sent him afield. Rome did not become his permanent home until he had reached his mid-thirties, and full citizenship was not granted him for twenty more years. A second reason is that at least during the early, unwealthy years of his residence in Rome, he had a vested interest in Greek letters and literature, for teaching them was his bread and oil. To augment his income he moonlighted as a poet, serving an occasional patron. His earliest poetic productions may well have been adaptations of tragedies to fill the stage left empty by the death of Livius and Naevius's exile. A third reason is that at some time during his life he met and absorbed some of the Empedoclean, Orphic, and Pythagorean ideas long current in the culturally Greek south of his youth. Their commonly held doctrine of the immortality and transmigration of souls was used to support his claim in the *Annals'* proem that the soul of Homer had literally entered his body. Here, for purposes of establishing poetic credentials, he may have been paying lip service to mysticism, just as the bronze priests found it politic to assert they were the voices of *numen*. But his claim has the unbudgeability of true belief; he was a man who had persuaded himself that he was commissioned to make verses. The difference between poet and priests—between Ennius and Homer, for that matter—was the imputed source of the commission: Ennius's source was professional, rational, human, and that of the priests and epic ancestor, divine. The influence of Pythagorean science is anybody's guess, but it's worth a bit of guessing because it could—if it exists—help to account for Ennius's determined assault on Helicon. (No slouch he, waiting for the nine ladies to descend to him.)

One of the discoveries of Pythagoras (fl. 6th century B.C. in Magna Graecia) was the monochord, a demonstration—

perhaps theoretical rather than actual—that musical intervals, as they occurred in the tunes of his and earlier days, depended on arithmetic ratios which expressed the relation of the vibrating part of a string to the whole string. The existence of the ratios was the novelty of this discovery. Sequences of ratios were used to construct melodic scales. The intervals, without this conscious arithmetic rationale, had already developed in Greek music, which has been described as "neither a linguistic nor a tonal art but the craft of composing *song*, considered as a unified entity."[33] This is not to suggest that the Greek poet-musicians were overtly mathematical composers or that Homer was a flesh and blood computer; given the stringed instruments of their times, the development of the intervals was a natural outcome of applied imagination. Very roughly, in Greek practice, voice and instrument, verb and melody were enclosed in a single system comprised of rhythm, or a patterned flow of sounds of long and short duration; of pitch, or the rise and fall of sound; and of amplitude, or the loudness and softness of sound. A sort of Morse Code (rhythm) sent in high and low frequencies (pitch), decibel level (amplitude) not necessarily altered. When this Greek Muse-art ceased to be always sung and came to have purely spoken forms, principles derived from the combined tone-word system still governed it. The question that has tempted philological speculation is, How did Ennius manage to apply its alien, quantitative, musical conventions to a language with rather different emotional effects and sound properties, with pronounced stress accents in particular? The question that tempts me is, Why? The answer may be simply that Ennius, making the unavoidable comparison, found the available Latin conventions to be pretty sorry things. But back to Pythagoras. The ratios and sequences of ratios found in music seemed to crop up everywhere, from the proportions— scales—of earthly temples to the movements of planets. The cosmological leap that followed seems foreordained: the Music of the Spheres. A rhythmic arithmetic that ordered the natural phenomena, tides and seasons and turning stars, and governed the neaps and springs of human fortunes as well. A single, indestructible, supra-audible mechanism behind all appearances.

I'd like to propose an Ennian theorem: Ennius was a mathematical poet who applied the principles of Greek music to his Latin because they best expressed the perfect proportions, the at last effable order, of the one eternal verity. Axiom from history: the proem to the *Annals* shows that Ennius, if not the compleat Pythagorean, was more than in passing familiar with Pythagorean ideas. Postulates from current thought: the source of poetic inspiration is man's need to adjust to natural and social stress, and poetry's function is to satisfy this need through the presentation of symbols that connect human feelings to perceptions of events-people-things. We are given an original identity between Greek meter and Greek musical measure, and we are also given the Pythagorean assumption that music and mathematics interdependently echo the vibrating truths of heaven and earth. It may be noted, too, that the word *numeri* was used in Ennius's lifetime to mean not only numbers but astronomy, musical measures, and verses. The proof of the theorem is fragile because not one Ennian poem can be read whole and thus put dispute to rest. But a few of the *Annals'* longer passages have recently been analyzed in attempts to show that the narrative can be divided according to its alternations between description:action or objectivity: subjectivity and that these alternations—number of lines with one effect:number of lines with the other—yield almost perfect Pythagorean ratios, especially The Golden Mean—.618.[34] In light of the poet's known acquaintance with Pythagoreanism, it seems that these analyses may be valid in spite of the fact that we have only as many lines as later authors wished to quote. And it seems that Ennius may indeed have used musical and mathematical concepts as they are embodied in meter and structural proportion in order to lift his *Annals* to the rarefied heights of absolute truth and to bring that truth within range of human ears. Which is not to say that an audience would consciously hear such structuring; it would have been to the poet's delight that meter imposed the surgent mathematicomusical rhythm of nature on the words and lines and that proportion imposed it on narrative. Together meter and proportion seem meant by the poem's creator to transform a need for history into the audible experience of a destiny that the Romans as a people could resist no more than the sun can resist rising. Perhaps Ennius transformed that need into a visible experience, too. For, there is something literally cinematic about reading and hearing ancient epic: ondriving motion inherent in meter + motion in the narration of onrolling events + alternation of panoramic description and zoom close-up on individual action = intentional movie for the third eye of the listener. The verb *canere* continues to work its old magic of bringing the thing-sung into actual being. In tuneful numbers, then, might not Ennius have sung that *romanitas* was not a sum of simple happenings but the sum of what had been foreordained to happen, QED?

In celebration the poetic changes took place. Once inspired, the poem was no longer thought to flow from noncorporeal sources nor was it put together mainly from traditional elements, sacred and popular. Experimentation, innovative adaptation, the obvious exercise of choice in techniques and resources, the existence of patronage and commissions, the roars of the critics—all signal poetry's growth into rational design. And in celebration the human changes took place. The anonymous singer became the named maker using all the skills at voluntary command.

180–100 B.C.: The poets of possibility rail and love.

Animo qui aegrotat videmus corpore hunc signum dare;
tum doloribus confectum corpus animo obsistere.

—Lucilius, 678–679

A sickness of mind, we see, makes its mark on flesh;
racked with pains, that flesh then ravages the mind.

The poetry of possibility found its first strong literary appearance in satire, later in erotic verse. In its earliest written form satire has only milk teeth. The element of Fescennine ridicule that later infuses it is present but dominated by the smorgasbord aspect. The luck of Naevius, who wrote the oldest surviving line of personal opinion, gives the reason. When the early iron poet's two taskmasters, self and state, were in opposition, publication could still bring punishment. Naevius composed a saturnian slur on the powerful Metelli family: *Fato Metelli Romae fiunt consules* (*Varia*, 2). The line has a forked tongue and can be read two ways, neither of them flattering: By fate alone the Metelli become consuls at Rome, or To Rome's misfortune the Metelli become consuls. For this impudence Naevius was jailed and later, quite unrehabilitated, sent into exile in Africa, where he died. Ennius, more cautious, is credited with regularizing satire's literary form. The remaining snaggles of Ennian satire point up the form's ancestral miscellaneousness; the poet used a mixed platter of meters and subjects that fragments show as ranging from story and Aesopian fable to jibes at such stock figures of fun as the too-clever trickster and the dinner guest who cleans not only his plate but his host's pantry. Ennius's tone is generally colloquial, though some of the humor seems a bit forced and fangless: "That turpitudissimest simian beast, how similar he is to us" (*Saturae*, 23).

But fifty years after Ennius's day of positive patriotism, the ecology of the poem—the relationship of its paraworld to the real world—had been altered. The Republic was rotten, suffering a metastasis of malignant problems whose seed was the practice of predatory economics on an increasingly grand scale. The Republican system was now a shell of the ideal of union, and it concealed a crazy spiderweb of personal intrigues. It was to linger feebly until Octavian, who was to become Augustus Caesar, won sole control of Rome's vast physical remains in 30 B.C. and undertook the construction of an empire. But hindsight places the beginning of the Republic's end in the

Second Punic War (218–202). The marks on the body social are plain to see. The war caused losses in the limited number of full citizens on whom the Republic depended to man its largely volunteer army and to fill the legislative and administrative offices for which citizens alone were eligible. The state tried to make good its losses. From the beginning of the second century on, Rome gradually granted the rights and duties of citizenship to its Italian allies, but in doing so it succeeded mainly in adulterating its ancient political order with variant elements. And from that time on it entrusted its defense more and more to a standing army whose swords were wielded for a leader as readily as for the society. As power settled in those men who commanded the loyalties of professional soldiers, armed force—or the threat of force—superseded due political process with increasing frequency. The Second Punic War also exhausted Rome's treasuries, and the state was obliged to seek fresh revenues. Africa, Greece, Spain, Gaul, Asia—each military drive for funds depleted moneys at hand and led to new shortages and then to renewed attempts to balance payments. Tax levies enacted to fill public coffers vanished into the purses of provincial administrators. The economic damage was not to be repaired at home. For, Hannibal's long occupation of the Italian countryside had brought a death to the land. Crops were destroyed, farmland devastated. The free, middle-class smallholders whose diversified produce had traditionally fueled the Roman engine were dispossessed, and they swarmed, with demobbed soldiers, into the cities where there was no work, no tradition, no sustenance. Aristocrats grabbed the deserted land, consolidated their holdings into broad estates, and, working them with cheap slave labor, began to raise the two crops—olives and grapes—that hardscrabble soil could most easily support. The grain for daily bread had to be imported. The riots and slave insurrections of the period were bloody screams for reform. Some attempts were made to alleviate the people's wretchedness and disorientation. Xenophobia rising and falling like an intermittent fever, traditionalists of

Cato's stripe, who longed for a return to supposedly simpler days and the ways of their ancestors, passed sumptuary laws and enacted legislation to expel Greek philosophers and their unsettling questions and to bar Asiatic cults with their glittering, symbolismically empty gods. These efforts were tantamount to barring the city gates after the admission of a Trojan horse. Liberals, like the idealistic Gracchi, established land redistribution and welfare policies that included make-work projects and a food-dole program. The projects were perfume, not soap, and the stink remained. The food dole brought economic chaos as the state for years sold grain to the poor at half its cost. To Rome's misfortune, the senate, in whose power lay the institution of lasting reforms, had become the hereditary fief of the old aristocracy, who were also often the owners of the huge estates and the trustees, as well, of the tax-collecting porkbarrel. The greater the profits in status quo, the narrower their interests in undercutting the bases of personal power.

In the last two centuries of the Republic, then, society was again polarized. Not between freeborn patricians and plebeians as before, but between a few princes and a multitude of paupers, both free and enslaved and neither enabled by circumstance to exercise choice. Rome had not found the golden mean between liberty and voluntary acceptance of limits to liberty on which a system of self-government succeeds. The individualism gradually let loose in earlier centuries became the antagonist of general reorganization. It rewarded strength with strength to the increasing detriment of the weak. And the pains of the body social manifested themselves in Roman minds. Belief still insisted that the good old ways were the best. But the realities of the day were unemployment, hunger and physical lassitude on the one hand, corruption and moral torpor on the other. There was a desperate loss of popular confidence in the connections that the state had created between men and men. Private selfishness on the part of Rome's leaders overwhelmed the ideal of public service, and an arid smugness supplanted the pride in heritage and national achievement that Ennius was satisfied to sing. It was again time to make poetic truth of what was, not what had been. The state in senescence was powerless to muzzle savage song.

Enter Lucilius. Born about 180 B.C. to a native middle-class Latin family who lived on the southwestern border of Latium, he died at Naples about 102. He was a long-time resident of Rome though never a citizen, a gentleman soldier who served in Spain under Scipio Aemilianus—later his probable patron, and a great-uncle to Pompey the Great. And he wears laurels as the man who defined satire as we now understand it. Horace in his own satires named Lucilius as the man who "rubbed the city in much salt" (*Satires*, I.x.3–4) and "first dared to compose songs in this fashion and peel off the skin in which each man walked, shining outwardly though rotten within" (the same, II.i.62–63).

The thirty books of Lucilius's *saturae* constitute, even in their fragmentation, a remarkable omnium-gatherum. Miscellaneous anecdotes jostle memorial epigrams in dialect to his slaves; a travelogue on a journey to the Strait of Messina rubs unheroic hexameters with a takeoff on an extortion trial; serious and dull metrical treatises on spelling and grammar mingle higgledy-piggledy with parodies on the *Odyssey* and contemporaneous Roman tragedies. The grab-bag idea is still apparent, but it has been displaced by the poet's anger at the follies of his times. Institutions and individuals alike are skewered on his low, wicked humor. Law court or rivals in love, heavenly lusts or mundane gluttony, nothing is sacred but the poet's own integrity, and sometimes he stands back and takes a poke at that, too.

It is in Lucilian satire that one first sees the reasons for the emergence of the mode of possibility in Latin literature. In craftsmanship Lucilius's poems were lowflown. Horace had apt words for the elder satirist's faults: his "verses run with stumbling feet" (the same, I.x.1) and he was "garrulous" and "too lazy to take the trouble of writing correctly" (the same, I.iv.12–13), although he was also "funny and urbane and more polished than crude as a creator of songs untouched by Greek influences" (the same, I.x.64–66). (Horace meant that the *type* of poetry was not influenced by Greece; Lucilius did employ Greek meters and latinize many Greek words.) But in spite of the technical weaknesses of his work, Lucilius was the poet unafraid, often identifying himself by name in his lines. And in him the poetic potential of the form began to be realized. It was the necessary complement to hymnsinging and celebration. Laughter releases the terrors of dying and impotence just as well as do ritual acts or daily adherence to an ethical code. Possibility was also the adversary of the other modes, an agent of revolution that could cut a man out of the common herd and press him toward self-directed thoughts and acts equivalent to a questioning of his own existence. Lewd, sentimental, serious, raging, light—whatever the tone, Lucilian satire was the voice of opposition. It spoke to people colloquially and informally. Where the poetries of survival and celebration dealt with people in terms of their similarities, *satura* gave Lucilius and poets to follow not only an eye for introspection but a means of treating every man as unique—inhabiting a body whose lumps and hollows were not quite like anybody else's, and tangled in his own peculiar net of feud and friendship, and struck by love and joy and hate and despair in proportions special to himself. And where survival poetry did not refer to man in any other than the collective sense, where celebration evoked supertruths that can only obliquely be seen as the products or paradigms of many tiny participations—war described or general eulogized, the single footsoldier and his everyday virtues to be imagined—Lucilian satire at its best could, in singling out the peculiarities of one man, move from small matters to large ones and suggest a condition of mankind. And suggest, too, that the condition was not an everlasting one but rather a present truth that could be turned into tomorrow's lie by an act of will. Most significant, with Lucilius, the Latin poem was directed upon the second of poetry's two maximal themes. The first, as illustrated by the poetries of survival and celebration, is that of man's mortality, the must-be-dones, the

obligatory way between darkness and darkness. The second is
that of love, the may-be-dones, the flowers that may be planted
or the mantraps dug and staked along that way. In Lucilius love
presents its nightside. But the scorn and almost violent vul-
garity that pepper his lines measure the capaciousness of a
freely given concern for the people as much as they do the
decadence of that people's second-century temper.

> Aufugit mi animus; credo, ut solet, ad Theotimum
>   devenit. . . .
> . . . quid ago? da, Venus, consilium.
>
> > —Q. Lutatius Catulus, consul in 102 B.C.
> > quoted by Aulus Gellius, work cited, XIX.ix.14

> My soul has run away. I think it's gone, as it's
>   accustomed, to Theotimus.
> . . . What to do? Venus, give your wise advice.

The oldest surviving erotic verses—the products, it seems,
of avocational poets—are loveless stuff. They were written as
the second century waned, and their inspiration can be directly
plumbed in extant Greek epigrams. What dry infatuations are
proclaimed! The poets—poetasters—adored the sonorities of
Latin, the schooled decencies of Alexandrian style, and the
game of mating one to the other more than they loved the
Theotimuses to whom the bons mots flew. Even the homosexu-
ality implied in the above quotation is imitation Greek.

But these are merely the obvious conclusions. For, the epi-
grams were in their frivolous fashion as experimental as Nae-
vian and Ennian epic, as necessary as Lucilius's satires. Though
Greek models had long been available for adaptation and the
grammarians hint that there were prior Latin expressions of
Eros, the epigrams mark the first real penetration of Latin
by the short snappy poem and its special meters. And conceits
conventional in Alexandrian mouths became radical in a Ro-
man context; the traditionalist of an earlier age could not, for
example, have imagined comparing mortal beauty to that of

deity and finding deity wanting. He could not, in the first place, have imagined god in man's image. Alexandria can be identified as the style-Muse, but the Muses of inspiration were Roman: the conditions already sketched that permitted—were impotent to stop—the publication of either satire or erotic verses, however veiled the latter in see-through Hellenophilia. The epigrams are the obverse of the Lucilian coin, day to his night, tenderness to his ferocity. Like his poems they ask the tacit question posed by the times: If the ancient numinous connection between men and nature and the newer connections legislated between men and men have failed, how may one guard oneself from chaos? The answer suggested by Lucilius and the epigrammatists is: In the reciprocated care of one person for one other.

But satires and epigrams could make truth only out of the ambiguities furnished by the times. Care? Or social organization worn to its simplest, most personally rewarding but least efficient nub—the group-of-two? Individualism? Or retreat to a group-of-one relationship with a mirror? Chaos came on like a barbarian. However psychosomatically necessary its symbolizations of human feeling—its connection-making— the poetry of possibility could offer no practical weapons for forestalling chaos's victory. It merely spotlighted the Republic's predicament. Yet it did perform practical services to future poetry. It legitimatized topics and techniques. It created new explosions on the frontiers of Latin. Its provocative expressions of opinion helped to protect through art a core of individualism—the will to action not reaction, the ability to make choices—through the dark years when its political exercise invited assassination. On Lucilian iron were founded the golden satires of Horace, the silver ones of Persius, Juvenal, and Martial, Dryden's *Absalom and Achitophel*, Pope's *Dunciad* and *Rape of the Lock*, and some of Ted Hughes's black *Crow* songs. The epigrammatic trivialists were Catullus *in utero*, and Ovid and Propertius, and Pound therefore. They were proto-Goliards singing love-in-the-spring. They were the earliest Romans to say *confiteor*, I confess. And, with

Lucilius, they were the first to place *ego et tu* at the heart of the paraworld.

Odi et amo. . . .

—Catullus, 85

For the end of my myth, a set of perhapses. Perhaps the preclassical fragments—Salian hymns and shards of The Twelve Tables through Lucilius and the epigrams—furnish clues to the overall evolution of Western poetry from words received like medicine dreams to fully voluntary creations for which a named maker is accountable even, in the earliest stages of accountability, unto death. For which he accepts internal creative responsibility. Perhaps the fragments show a shift of emphasis and purpose from creature survival in the inescapable grasp of death to illumination of the possibilities of love— the lending of individual meaning to survival. And show a development of the preclassical poem as an instrument of symbolic service to small group, larger group or state, and individual in that chronological sequence. And show poetry's separation from religion and its emergence as an unaccompanied verbal art. And illustrate a maturation of the poetic impulse from numinous, Camenaeal nape-prickle to intentional act. And point to the physical and mental maturation of the archaic singer-performer, who was a real child or an adult thinking inescapably in the child's magical terms, into the maker who was a man possessed of—by—an alphabet, formal tools of logic, and the power of choice.

But, not everything changed or grew. The times, not the man, made the soul of song or poem; the man made evocative form within the limits of his own experience and genius, with the techniques and ideas conceivable in the context of his times. No matter what name was given it—Camenae, Muses, manic ecstasy, or sane inborn gift—inspiration was always orientation-need. Singer or poet, the job was constant—to create paraworlds apprehendable by other people. The predicament was constant—that poems were judged continually by critic, poet, and society alike on the grounds of a nonexistent practical utility. The verb was constant—*cano,* I sing, and the act of singing brought the paraworld from nothingness into being. And always—above, beyond, within—*numen* of course perdured. Perdures.

Here ends the myth. But one question is still to be answered. Song and poem, what is the now in them?

3
PLASMATA

A<small>LL TRANSLATION</small> poses problems of truth. To which of the elements that formed the original work shall fidelity be given? At the expense of what else? Within a text, meaning, style, sound, ancestry in art all claim attention. Outside it stand the demands of historical and literary milieux, the author's place in both, his intent, its real and imputed sources, and the people for whom he made poem. Then, these coefficients and the many others duly weighted and reset or rejected, truth further depends on the translator's purpose, be it production of a trot, art's reflection, its re-creation, or loading a handy packmule with the translator's own ideas. I admit to the last. And I hope for re-creation in forms appropriate to this year—*our* now-context—not of the broken bronze and iron verses themselves but of the spark that once quickened them into poem.

In a sense I perpetrate a fraud. Any translation by its very nature cannot take a reader to the original poem; the translation process stands like wavy glass between the artifact and the reader's apprehension of it. And I have tackled Ennius-on-war with an irony that he surely did not write into his lines, and Lucilius-on-human-folly with visions of New York city heaped in my head. But, in another sense, there is no fraud at all. A poem is the visible-audible verbal resolution of a stressful encounter between poet and someone-something-some event else, and a *plasma*-poem is an artifact from my own encounter with bronze and iron.

For the making of *plasmata*, the very existence of the fragments, the lingering life they suffer on uncut pages in library stacks, is taken as an historical core on which to mold might-have-beens and maybes and as-ifs. From the collections of fragments I have taken lines and regrouped them—epic fragment, for example, with a scrap from tragedy—according to the themes they suggest and the pictures they paint on my mind. Spirits numinous and anthropomorphic yield to their attributes; Latin grammar to the sense of the English; and living performance to the still white page. No attempt to re-create prosody has been made. Being neither ologist nor ographer but a relay station on the way to the poem-spark's apprehension, I assume license to try the repair job with imagination and intuition. Possible rearrangements are, of course, as many as there may be survivors of the *Gallic Wars* who wish to mull the fragments now and tomorrow and the century after that. There are many fragments I have regretfully not been able to use. They are left with love to anybody who wants them.

And what idea does my packmule bear? Humpty Dumpty cannot be restored to pristine orotundity. But he can be patched. Not history but life repeats itself, regardless of circumscription by clock and landscape and tool and language. The articulation of the bones, the fluent blood speak about the inescapable, basic aspects of being alive that people share, no matter the year or place, as they share air to breathe and earth to walk upon. We're born, we die. Interim stomachs growl, eyelids grow heavy, hearts perform every cliché acrobatic. Cultures change, as do the responses they teach. The hideousness of war and the pain of exile do not. Nor does the hope of love. Nor, even, the politics of poetry. The greatness of the bronze and iron poems—old in time yet vulnerably young in craft—is that they voice now and severally the things the blood and bones have always known. But let the spark sing itself.

BRONZE

Sed illa mutari vetat religio et consecratis utendum est.

—Quintilian, *Institutio Oratoria,* I.vi.41

But religion forbids that these songs be altered, and they must
be used as wholly sacred things.

SURVIVAL

YEARSONGS OF THE LEAPING PRIESTS

<table>
<tr><td>FROM THE
FULLNESS OF
WINTERNIGHTS</td><td>When you shouted   white skyripper
we shuddered beneath you
Why was it right   bright blade of thunder
to wound us with misfortunes</td></tr>
<tr><td>A NEWBORN
LIGHT</td><td>Dayblaze   its blue house   chant them
Day of days   homing   shiver praise</td></tr>
</table>

Dark seeds in earth   spring lightward
there is a world to see
Closed gate of winter   swing open
old is made new again
Sun in the year's door   live again
strong to lift death from us

<table>
<tr><td>AND AT SONG'S
END LET MY
NAMES SOUND</td><td>Ironspear and spear of wheat
Bonesmith and smiter of death
End and beginning of breath</td></tr>
</table>

—after the Salian hymns

Texts

Volumnia[1]

Quome tonas, Leucesie,
prae tet tremonti.
quor libet, Curis,
decstumum tonare?[2]

Lucia[1]

Divom templa cante,
divom deo supplicate.[2]

Conse, ulod oriese:
omnia tuere,
adi, Patulci, coi isse:
Sancus Ianes Cerus es.
Duonus Ianus vevet
po melios, eu, recum.[2]

nominaque ex- Mamuri
tremo carmina Mamuri
nostra sonent Mamuri[3]

HYMN FOR SEEDTIME AND
A SAFE HARVEST

now   life in the houses of flesh   help us
now   love in our hearts' hearths   help us
now   fleshfires   help us

let not war nor sickness   slay hope   at the year's turning
nor abortion nor stillbirth   waste hope   with the months' passing
     nor blood   rust hope   at this moon's waning

guard fiercely   the pale sprout that roots   in the tender earth
guard fiercely   the soft calf that swims   in the dark before birth
guard fiercely   the red life that screams   into this world

sower   in turn   sow
semen   in turn   flow
seed   in turn   grow

lifeforce   that hardens the swords of men   help us
lifeforce   that ripens and bursts in women   help us
littledeath   that bears the survival of life   help us

yes   yes   yes   yesyes

—after the Arval chant

Text

Enos, Lases, iuvate,
enos, Lases, iuvate,
enos, Lases, iuvate.
neve lue rue, Marmar, sins incurrere in pleoris,
neve lue rue, Marmar, sins incurrere in pleoris,
neve lue rue, Marmar, sers incurrere in pleoris.
satur fu, fere Mars: limen sali: sta berber,
satur fu, fere Mars: limen sali: sta berber,
satur fu, fere Mars: limen sali: sta berber,
semunis alternei advocapit conctos,
semunis alternei advocapit conctos,
semunis alternei advocapit conctos.
enos, Marmor, iuvato,
enos, Marmor, iuvato,
enos, Marmor, iuvato.
triumpe, triumpe, triumpe, triumpe, triumpe.

IRON

Mirum videtur quod sit factum iam diu?

—Livius Andronicus, *Tragoediae*, 15

Does it seem a marvel because it was made long ago?

'nam divina Monetas filia docuit

—the same, *Odissia*, 30

for the Muse, holy daughter of Memory, has taught them

CELEBRATIONS

NAEVIUS
270?–201 B.C.

Quid si taceat? Dum videat, tam sciat. . . .
quid scriptum sit.

—Ex incertis fabulis, 13–14

What if he is silent? While one sees, one may still know
what has been written.

INVOCATION

Nine daughters of shining day, choired sisters
your honeysweet singing
I do not know the way, but you know it all

Text

Novem Iovis concordes filiae sorores,
Bellum Poenicum, 1

suavisonum melos
Tragoediae, 35

Ignotae iteris sumus, tute scis.
Ibid., 36

THE PIONEERS

When my husband's father saw vultures gathering
ominously in our quadrant of the sky, he set out
our store of household goods upon a table and said
    his prayers,
and he slaughtered for a last feast my heifer calf
with the hide of gold.

We cried, my husband's mother and I, when she locked
    the door.
The night veiled our flooded eyes.

And we carried away our belongings, bowls, kettles,
one glass goblet that used to turn whitegold in the
    sunlight,
and freshly-laundered clothes, pomander-sweet.
My best crocus-gold dress was packed; I wore the black
that is saved for funerals.

I was husbanded to the ship as my heifer had walked
    to death,
not prodded but hand-led.

The Westerlies plumped our sails, pushed us over roiled
seas to a halfmoon bay where the winds shatter granite
and a pineblack shore lies locked in the sky's lead
    cave.
Strange people shied behind the trees quick as fawns or
    ghosts
without our craft of war.

We raised small steeples of hands and gave thanks to
    God.
Our course is followed by many men.

Text

Postquam avem aspexit in templo Anchisa,
sacra in mensa Penatium ordine ponuntur;

immolabat auream victimam pulchram.

Bellum Poenicum, 2-4

Amborum uxores
noctu Troiad exibant capitibus opertis,
flentes ambae abeuntes lacrimis cum multis.

Ibid., 5-7

Ubi foras cum auro illic exibant,

Ibid., 10

puram pulchramque ex auro vestem citrosam.

Ibid., 11

Ferunt pulchras creterras, aureas lepistas.

Ibid., 12

pallis patagiis crocotis malacis mortualibus

Tragoediae, 39

sine ferro ut pecua manibus ad mortem meant.

Ibid., 45

Passo velo vicinum, Aquilo, me hinc in portum fer
foras!

Ibid., 21

⟨confrages⟩ . . . in montes ubi venti frangebant locum.

Ex incertis fabulis, 40

hemisphaerium ubi conca⟨vo⟩
caerulo septum stat.

Varia

. . . silvicolae homines bellique inertes

Bellum Poenicum, 18

manusque susum ad caelum sustulit suas rex
Amulius divisque gratulatur.

Ibid., 21-22

Eorum sectam sequuntur multi mortales.

Ibid., 8

EPITAPH

If spirit may mourn for flesh,
then mourn, Poem, for your poet.
He lies in death's hoard of silence,
and living men are bereft of words.

Text

Immortales mortales si foret fas flere
flerent divae Camenae Naevium poetam.
Itaque postquamst Orchi traditus thesauro,
obliti sunt Romae loquier lingua latina.

ENNIUS
239–169 B.C.

THE YEARS, THE TRAGEDIES, VARIOUS UNCERTAINTIES, AND AN EPITAPH

Enni poeta salve qui mortalibus
versus propinas flammeos medullitus!

Saturae, 6–7

Your safety, Ennius, who drew your poems from bone's
red wine and passed them, set aflame, to thirsty men.

EVOCATION

Daughters of light
Muses whose heartbeats make the mountaintop tremble

once in dark forests the fauns and the prophets chanted
the unstudied songs the trees gave them
and knew no words else
nor thought to mount the steep track toward the sunlight

when I was sleeping, caught in the soft chains of dreaming,
Homer the maker entered me promising
your theme and your poems
shall shine in the minds of your people

and I have dared climb

Text

⟨Iovis . . . filiae⟩

Musae quae pedibus magnum pulsatis Olympum;

Annales, 1

quos olim Fauni vatesque canebant,
quom nequ Musarum scopulos. . . .
. . . nec dicti studiosus quisquam erat ante hunc

Ibid., 232–234

somno leni placidoque revinctus

Ibid., 4

visus Homerus adesse poeta.

Ibid., 5

Nam populos. . .
. . . Italos res atque poemata nostra cluebunt.

Ibid., 2–3

Nos ausi reserare

Ibid., 235

PORTRAIT, PERHAPS, OF AN ELDER POET

A word said: Come.
 Many good freewheeling nights he's given me
meat and drink and food for thought. Tonight,
another sharing, though he'll be tired, daylight
and self spent:
 the world wants words to be ruled by,
guide lines read carefully
 in crowded parks, in hallowed halls.
But nights he is boldly his own man.
 Solemn talk and small talk and jokes and
he speaks out vividly, no caution, black words
spewed, and candid words, whatever
 his will; my tongue is safely locked on
many trusts, secret letch, gladness set free.
Yet, genius in him, darkless, no words persuade
that darkness creates light.
 Learned, learning, truth possessed, he is
a man I'm easy with,
 wordsure, content to be himself, at peace,
insightful, measuring

our exacting times with the exact few terms,
holding fast to many antique forms an age in ruins
made, holding forth new modes for old truths
told by old men, upholding
    spirit's laws with laws of mortal dust.
His skill, delivering words well; knowing
    when to let words rest unsaid, his power.
Mid controversies he compels me: Come. So be it.

Text

Haece locutus vocat quocum bene saepe libenter
mensam sermonesque suos rerumque suarum
comiter inpertit, magnam cum lassus diei
partem trivisset de summis rebus regendis,
consilio indu foro lato sanctoque senatu;
quoi res audacter magnas parvasque iocumque
eloqueretur sed cura, malaque et bona dictu
evomeret si qui vellet tutoque locaret;
quocum multa volup ac gaudia clamque palamque,
ingenium quoi nulla malum sententia suadet
ut faceret facinus levis aut malus; doctus fidelis
suavis homo facundus, suo contentus, beatus,
scitus, secunda loquens in tempore, commodus, verbum
paucum, multa tenens antiqua, sepulta vetustas
quae facit, et mores veteresque novosque, tenens res
multorum veterum, leges divumque hominumque,
prudenter qui dicta loquive tacereve posset.
Hunc inter pugnas Servilius sic conpellat.

                              Annales, 210–227

THE WEST

There is a land men have thought of as The West,

an earth held in the womb of hope for seeding.
Many people have quickened it, rich free men,

men nameless in the shadows of poverty, that they
might perfect their days with unanimity forever.

They sailed over seas calm as sungilded stone.
Ships crowded on ships, wake on green wake lit
hissing saltfires. Or furies of wind drove them,
and the galeswollen salt raged hugely with ships.
Long coasts echoed the sounds of a human surf
when the filled ships were emptied and men surged
westward and westward to fulfill the empty land.

They slashed through tall trees and conquered them
with axes. Ancient white oaks fell, and red oaks,
ashtrees splintered before them, tall firs crashed,
and proud pines, and everywhere, everywhere dry
thunders of leaves, lightnings of splitting wood.

The sun shone gold on them. And appletrees came
to bloom, grapevines grew plump with glad rounds
of wine-to-be, berrycanes bowed red with riches,
grain sprouted greengold, all the earth flowered,
springs flowed, grasses clothed pastures, children
were born to new light where an eagle in unveering
flight defeated the wind. Some dreams are true,

but not all of them. Autumn followed the easy time.
Snowknives flew. Cruelties of ice crushed strong men
and men whose hollowed guts snarled hunger and men
sleek with hoarding. No man spoke with honesty.
Sickness killed some of them. Others died of war:

All life must somehow end; knowing this, old men
sent their sons not to forage but support survival
with feasts of death. Metal clashed, bones splin-
tered, the earth sweated blood. And the sons died.
Corpse crowded on corpse, grave on mass grave.
In spring the leaves bloomed red. Icefree rivers
bled freshets of red filth down to the shining sea.

Seeking, finding, dying, grieving—these were done
long ago. On the antique hopes and whitened bones

of many people a nation now stands, its fertile
plains and sprawling skyward cities their monuments.

Why are my thoughts today alive with sorrow?

Text

Est locus, Hesperiam quam mortales perhibebant,
                                        Annales, 24

                        Saturno
quem Caelus genuit.   *Ibid.,* 27–28

                        Saturnia terra
                        Ibid., 26

quod bonus et liber populus   *Spuria?* 31

Multi alii adventant, paupertas quorum obscurat nomina.
                                        Tragoediae, 53

'Aeternum seritote diem concorditer ambo.'
                                        Annales, 110

Verrunt extemplo placide mare marmore flavo;
caeruleum spumat sale conferta rate pulsum.
                                        Ibid., 372–373

                        furentibus ventis
                        Ibid., 561

                'et aequora salsa veges ingentibus ventis.'
                                        Tragoediae, 374

                        ratibus fremebat
imber Neptuni.   *Annales,* 534–535

Litora lata sonunt   *Ibid.,* 377

navibus explebant sese terrasque replebant.
                                        Ibid., 540

Incedunt arbusta per alta, securibus caedunt.
Percellunt magnas quercus, exciditur ilex,

fraxinus frangitur atque abies consternitur alta,
pinus proceras pervortunt; omne sonabat
arbustum fremitu silvai frondosai.

> *Ibid.*, 181–185

Caelum nitescere, arbores frondescere,
vites laetificae pampinis pubescere,
rami bacarum ubertate incurvescere,
segetes largiri fruges, florere omnia,
fontes scatere, herbis prata convestirier.

> *Tragoediae*, 157–161

'Tu produxisti nos intra luminas oras.

> *Annales*, 121

et densis aquila pinnis obnixa volabat
vento quem perhibent Graium genus aera lingua.

> *Ibid.*, 151–152

⏑ Aliquot somnia vera ⟨sunt⟩ sed omnia non necesse est.

> *Ex comoediis*, 427

Aestatem autumnus sequitur, post acer hiems it.

> *Annales*, 395

viresque valentes
contudit crudelis hiems   *Ibid.*, 514–515

nam neque irati neque blandi quicquam sincere sonunt.

> *Tragoediae*, 112

Hos pestis necuit, pars occidit illa duellis.

> *Annales*, 476

⟨liberos⟩
ego cum genui tum morituros scivi et ei rei sustuli:
praeterea ad Troiam cum misi ob defendendam Graeciam,
scibam me in mortiferum bellum non in epulas mittere.

> *Tragoediae*, 319–322

ut nos nostri liberi
defendant pro nostra vita morti occumbant obviam.

> *Ibid.*, 140–141

Aes sonit franguntur hastae terra sudat sanguine.

Ibid., 196

Exaequant tumulis tumulos ac mortibus mortes
accumulant. *Spuria?* 16–17

russescunt frundes

Annales, 241

Miscent foede flumina candida sanguine sparso.

Spuria? 14

maerentes flentes lacrumantes commiserantes

Ibid., 40

Factum est iam diu.

Tragoediae, 24

Moribus antiquis res stat Romana virisque.

Annales, 467

'Testes sunt Campi Magni. *Scipio*, 14

Urbes magnas atque imperiosas

Varia, 21

'Sed, quid ego hic animo lamentor?

Annales, 196

THE BROTHERS

—And who hopes to rule over these square miles?
To decide rule by force is the habit of beasts.
With peace, not violence, let the land be served—

Caring with harsh care,
            coveting one kingdom,
they keep twin vigils
            for omens, for visions.
On the hill where the day rises,
            solitude: give me
one sign in the cloudfold of heaven.

On the vesper height, prayer:
Let there be sign on sign
        in the sunplowed heavens.

Stay with the harvest, follow the herds:
        that was their quarrel.

Valley-deep, a vigil of kinsmen:
        which one shall win us?
They watch tense as racecrowds
        craving beginnings,
every impatient eye drawn
        to the starting gates—
soon a swiftness will break from those jaws,
        soon a decision;
and keep watch like worshippers,
        tongues mute with awe, with
not knowing: to which one
        the victory, the prize, the kingdom?

Nightfall blinded
        the sun's pale staring.

In the dawn's gate, a dazzle,
        an upthrusting light,
and lured from the pierced height
        the bird prayed-for plummets,
its winged shadow raking
        the sun's rising gold.
And is joined, tier on tier,
        by heavenly hosts, a rapture
of eagles, hurtling home
        to the sun's risen heart.

To the heart of one sight:
        it is sure: to the sower
the tokens of kingship, its rights and powers,
        its tangible earth.

—The people have belted the fields with walls.

Time and again the shepherd approaches them:
'You trust stones more than your plow-callused hands!'

'Kings mark no bond of brotherhood nor private faith.
No man, however much provoked, may taunt us with
        impunity.
Nor you, and you shall pay hot penalties of blood.'

The people stand above their king in this respect,
that they may cry. Honor forbids him tears—

Text

Et qui sperat Romae regnare Quadratae?
Annales, 123

nam vi depugnare sues stolidi soliti sunt.
Ibid., 106

'Astu non vi sum summam servare decet rem,

Ibid., 105

Curantes magna cum cura tum cupientes
regni dant operam simul auspicio augurioque;
in Murco Remus auspicio sedet atque secundam
solus avem servat. At Romulus pulcher in alto
quaerit Aventino, servat genus altivolantum.
Certabant urbem Romam Remoramve vocarent.
Omnibus cura viris uter esset induperator:
expectant, veluti consul quom mittere signum
volt, omnes avidi spectant ad carceris oras
quam mox emittat pictis e faucibus currus:
sic expectabat populus atque ora *timebat*
dubius utri magni victoria sit data regni.
Interea sol albus recessit in infera noctis.
Exin candida se radiis dedit icta foras lux;
et simul ex alto longe pulcherrima praepes
laeva volavit avis, simul aureus exoritur sol.
Cedunt de caelo ter quattuor corpora sancta

avium, praepetibus sese pulchrisque locis dant.
Conspicit: inde sibi *ratus* Romulus esse propritim
auspicio regni stabilita scamna solumque.
Ibid., 80–100

Albani muris Albam Longam cinxerunt.
Spuria? 1

atque atque accedit muros Romana iuventus.
Annales, 529

'Iuppiter, ut muro fretus magis quamde manus vi!'
Ibid., 101

Nulla sancta societas
nec fides regni est.   *Ex fabulis incertis, 402–403*

'Nec pol homo quisquam faciet inpune animatus
hoc nec tu; nam mi calido dabis sanguine poenas.'
Annales, 102–103

Plebes in hoc regi antistat loco: licet
lacrumare plebi, regi honeste non licet.
Tragoediae, 235–236

ON AN ARMY OF OCCUPATION

Not knowing how to use time, time free, kills time:
harder work than working hard when there is hard work.
Occupying time, work set, no work in that, but yes,
purpose, zeal, a timelessness, a joy in mind and self.
Wasting time, not knowing what to want, self wastes.
So for us now, not home in peace, not on the battlefield,
we go forth, here there, arriving there, would go elsewhere:
self-defeat—no time for living, not yet time to die.

Text

Otio qui nescit uti ⟨quom otium est, in otio⟩
plus negoti habet quam quom est negotium in negotio;

nam cui quod agat institutumst non ullo negotio
id agit, id studet, ibi mentem atque animum delectat suum:
otioso in otio ⟨aeger⟩ animus nescit quid velit.
Hoc idem est; em neque domi nunc nos nec militiae sumus;
imus huc, hinc illuc; quom illuc ventum est, ire illinc lubet.
Incerte errat animus, praeterpropter vitam vivitur.

Tragoediae, 241–248

TO BE A MAN

To be a man is to become alive to truth and act—
to fight with guts and faith for it alone against all odds.
Freedom! Yours, who daily wear this bright hard courage.
Unmanned, you who cower captive to your dread of night.

Text

Sed virum vera virtute vivere animatum addecet
fortiterque innoxium stare adversum adversarios.
ea libertas est qui pectus purum et firmum gestitat;
aliae res obnoxiosae nocte in obscura latent.

Tragoediae, 308–311

ONE DAY OF WAR
A Sequence in Virtual Time

I: THE NIGHT WATCH

Here they stand watch in an ambush of moonshadow
cast by the sloping mountains where night is born

and soars up bearing its stars like bright eagles.

Some rest—those who trust courage—swordguarded,
mute, safe from fear's grip in their sheltering
longshields.

What hour does night's roundshield say it is?
The Big Dipper keeps ladling out stars.

Over there the mercenaries start bragging of luck,
yesterday's, tomorrow's, to hurry the festive day:

> Kill legions . . . strip the fat fields, take towns
> . . . or a woman, what luck's truer than a woman?

And over there others try to muzzle their gutgripes:

> When will there be a lull in fighting, when
> will hard war end? Our plows, our fields wait.

The sky slowly changes its huge guard of stars.

And there's the young lieutenant, sword buckled
over his heart and his soul on his smooth face:

> Soon it's to be life or death . . . either one
> means someone's harvest or old age shall ripen.
> Live, die, I'm not afraid. Father, fatherland . . .
> lifegiving earth . . . be safe.

The night marches on, armored in burning stars.

The freedom they shall fight for, may it last forever.

Text

Hic insidiantes vigilant, partim requiescunt
contecti gladiis, sub scutis ore faventes.

Annales, 403–404

montibus obstipis obstantibus unde oritur nox.

Ibid., 398

Nox quando mediis signis praecincta volabit,

Ibid., 400

Nec metus ulla tenet; freti virtute quiescunt.

Ibid., 478

Quid noctis videtur in altisono
caeli clipeo?

Temo superat

stellas sublime agitans etiam atque
etiam noctis iter.   *Tragoediae, 222–225*

   . . . fortunasque suas coepere latrones
inter se memorare.   *Annales, 481–482*

   festivum festinant diem *Ex fabulis incertis, 436*

   Quianam legiones caedimus ferro?
                                      Annales, 525

deque totondit agros laetos atque oppida cepit.
                                      Ibid., 524

mulierem; quid potius dicam aut verius quam mulierem?
                                      Tragoediae, 417

Aspectabat virtutem legionis suai
expectans si mussaret, 'quae denique pausa
pugnandi fieret aut duri finis laboris?'
                                      Annales, 333–335

Rastros dentiferos capsit causa poliendi
agri   *Ibid., 318–319*

Vertitur interea caelum cum ingentibus signis.
                                      Ibid., 205

Optima cum pulchris animis Romana iuventus
                                      Annales, 489

   succincti corda machaeris.
                                      Ibid., 491

   'tibi vita
seu mors in mundo est'   *Ibid., 458–459*

nobis unde forent fructus vitaeque propagmen.
                                      Ibid., 475

   Vivam an moriar nulla in me est metus.
                                      Tragoediae, 411

parentem et pa⟨triam . . .
   ⟩ sospitem.   *Ibid., 390–391*

terrai frugiferai   *Annales,* 564

Hinc nox processit stellis ardentibus apta.

Ibid., 332

'libertatemque, ut perpetuassit
quaeque axim   *Ibid.,* 320–321

II: DAWN

red sky at dawning

The morning star retreats, a paling fugitive.
The wheel looms, its bright spokes disclosing
the daycolors

heaven's broad blue field

this green field on earth
silver of spiderfloss

the black man-columns forming

Text

aere fulva

Annales, 440

Interea fugit albus iubar Hyperionis cursum.

Ibid., 559

Inde patefecit radiis rota candida caelum.

Ibid., 558

i caerula prata.

Ibid., 149

bussus araneae

Varia, 28

It nigrum campis agmen   *Annales*, 513

III: REVEILLE

> *Sun's up. Open your eyes, soldier.*
> *Dry the dreams from your brain.*
>
> I dreamed about my bluetick bitch.
> Chained, she'd caught the scent
> of something wild. She whimpered . . .
>
> *The signal has sounded.*
>
> and, deepmouthed, she bugled.
> No one dreams truth until he learns
> to know it with waking senses.
>
> *Today, live or die,*
> *you'll know what glory is.*
>
> Many years, many miles from home,
> I've fought hard battles. I know
> one day of war bears many hazards.
>
> *The order is issued: Stand firm;*
> *dig graves in enemy flesh.*
>
> The man who plans destruction
> for an enemy should know the enemy
> has planned the same for him.
>
> *Brave men are the lucky ones.*
>
> I know that luck runs out and
> no one's been lucky all his life.
> I have dreamed I was dead.

Text

Inde patefecit radiis rota candida caelum.

Annales, 558

'Pandite sultis genas et corde relinquite somnum.'

Ibid., 479

Quom sese exsiccat somno Romana iuventus

Ibid., 480

Veluti se quando vinclis venatica velox
apta solet si forte feras ex nare sagaci
sensit, voce sua nictit ululatque ibi acute.

Ibid., 339–341

Inde loci lituus sonitus effudit acutos

Ibid., 488

nec quisquam sophiam sapientia quae perhibetur
in somnis vidit prius quam sam discere coepit.

Ibid., 229–230

'Nunc est ille dies quom gloria maxima sese
nobis ostendat, si vivimus sive morimur.'

Ibid., 378–379

annos multos longinque ab domo
bellum gerentes summum summa industria.

Tragoediae, 83–84

'Multa dies in bello conficit unus . . .

Annales, 284

Decretum est stare ⟨et fossari⟩ corpora telis.

Ibid., 511

qui alteri exitium parat,
eum scire oportet sibi paratum pestem ut participet parem.

Tragoediae, 176–177

'Fortibus est fortuna viris data.

Annales, 254

et rursus multae fortunae forte recumbunt;
haudquaquam quemquam semper fortuna secuta est.

Ibid., 285–286

Nam videbar somniare med ego esse mortuum.
Epicharmus, 1

IV: MORNING

morning's arched immensity

sun that uplifts slow white heat toward meridian

Like oil sunlight glistens on seasoned troops,
their bodies signed with old battlescars. They have teethed
on swords, their hands are wise with killing, and ready.

No sound, no movement, a honed attention. Listen,
the general asks fortune to make this day fruitful . . .

FOR THE GLORY OF OUR GODS

FOR KING AND COUNTRY

FOR OUR RIGHT CAUSE

AND FOR OUR LIVES

Shieldgleam, spearglitter, sunwhetted blade,
the enemy, mustering, bristles with light.

Text

caeli ingentes fornices
Tragoediae, 387

Sol qui candentem in caelo sublimat facem
Ibid., 287

conque fricati oleo lentati adque arma parati.
Annales, 107

Insignita fere tum milia militum octo
duxit delectos, bellum tolerare potentes.
Ibid., 337–338

Sileteque et tacete atque animum advertite;
Audire iubet vos imperator   *Tragoediae,* 2–3

'Quod mihi reique fidei regno vobisque, Quirites,
se fortunatim feliciter ac bene vortat.
Annales, 112–113

Sparsis hastis longis campus splendet et horret.
Scipio, 6

Horrescit telis exercitus asper utrimque.
Annales, 380

V: TATTOO

A hortative trumpet shrieks Attack Attackattack.

Foot bruises foot and
       arms batter arms and
              man grinds man,

       the roundshields sound resound,
              spears whizz whistle keen,
                     a sword curves home, singing

              A hot curve of blood spurts,
                     trumpet blurts a last raucous
                     tattoo

              and the head
                     on its raw stumpneck
                            screams silence.

The eyes jerk, glitter in mocklife begging for light.

Text

At tuba terribili sonitu taratantara dixit.

Annales, 143

. . . ⟨hic⟩ pede pes premitur, armisque teruntur
arma . . .   ⟨viro vir⟩.

Ibid., 507–508

Tum clipei resonunt et ferri stridit acumen;

Ibid., 356

missaque per pectus dum transit striderat hasta.

Ibid., 357

. . . misso sanguine tepido tullii efflantes volant.

Tragoediae, 23

Quomque caput caderet, carmen tuba sola peregit
et pereunte viro raucus sonus aere cucurrit.

Annales, 499–500

Oscitat in campis caput a cervice revulsum
semianimesque micant oculi lucemque requirunt.

Ibid., 501–502

VI: NOON

flared nostrils pouring out firefloods of light
the horses that pull the sun conquer the noonpoint
and stop
stock
still

Nothing moves. Uncanny calm. The time, no time.
Skyspin and ocean's seething wildness, sun's flight,
rivers racing year in year out, all stand still, all
leaves hang mute, unmoved, this world without wind, this

lull in the frenzy

. . . commanders . . . rowelling words

FOR GODS gods and
FOR KING king and
FOR COUNTRY our countreee
EEEEEYAAH CUT cut gut gut gut

Cry echoes cry, a skysplitting stutter.

hollow hooves   dull detonations   pulverized earth
arms upraised   ironscud   sun gone dim

Running, the seas running, everywhere wild weather,
sky flickers forked light, southwind is rising,
eaglewind strikes squalling, gale in its craw,
and the seas where they grapple are upflung torn down, these

living lines surge
pulled to stormflood by anger

Text

funduntque elatis naribus lucem.

Annales, 560

sublime iter quadrupedantes flammam halitantes

Tragoediae, 189

Mundus caeli vastus constitit silentio
et Neptunus saevus undis asperis pausam dedit,
sol equis iter repressit ungulis volantibus,
constitere amnes perennes, arbores vento vacant.

Scipio, 1–4

pausam fecere fremendi.

Annales, 466

. . . horitatur . . . induperator

Ibid., 336

'Quod mihi reique fidei regno vobisque, Quirites,
se fortunatim feliciter ac bene vortat.

Ibid., 112–113

Heia machaeras!
Ibid., 523

Tollitur in caelum clamor exortus utrimque.
Ibid., 433

It eques et plausu cava concutit ungula terram.
Ibid., 429

Hastati spargunt hastas; fit ferreus imber.
Ibid., 281

Concurrunt veluti venti quom spiritus Austri
imbricitor Aquiloque suo cum flamine contra
indu mari magno fluctus extollere certant.
Ibid., 430–432

. . . ita mortales inter sese pugnant proeliant.
Tragoediae, 13

irarum effunde quadrigas
Annales, 550

VII: IRONSTORM

> Spearlightning stabs at him, pierces
> his shield, clinks on its metal studs.
> His helmet clangs with a thunder
> of struck brass. But not one spear
> of that ironstorm tears him; he breaks
> and shakes off the hard-driven rain.
> And is drenched by his own sweat.
> Can't catch enough breath.
> > Death
> plunges heavily into his side, his
> knees crush the ground. A cave
> of armor comes clattering over him;
> its rising clamor mewls on the wind.
> And the body that earth gave, earth
> will take back, wasting none of it.

Undique conveniunt velut imber tela tribuno:
configunt parmam, tinnit hastilibus umbo
aerato sonitu galeae, sed nec pote quisquam
undique nitendo corpus discerpere ferro;
semper abundantes hastas frangitque quatitque;
totum sudor habet corpus multumque laborat,
nec respirandi fit copia; praepete ferro
Histri tela manu iacientes sollicitabant.

Annales, 409–416

        nam me gravis impetus Orchi
percutit in latus.   *Ibid., 504–505*

      pinsunt terram genibus.   *Ibid., 342*

concidit et sonitum simul insuper arma dederunt.
                    Ibid., 417

Clamor ad caelum volvendus per aethera vagit.
                    Ibid., 421

          'terraque corpus
quae dedit ipsa capit neque dispendi facit hilum.
                  Ibid., 11–12

VIII: AFTERNOON

Butchery grows long, time short, daring gutters out.
The charge is blunted by a countercharge.
The line retreats.
          Dead tired.
              Run to earth.
And there are hunters everywhere.

The cadre, action-proved, falls back on words—
threats, exhortations—to strike a winning rage:

STOP MEWING LIKE WOMEN IN LABOR.
AMID WAR'S BLOOD AND SHIT MANHOOD IS BORN.

WHO WINS? THERE IS NO WINNER
WITHOUT A LOSER WHO ADMITS TO LOSS
AS LONG AS ONE OF US SURVIVES. . . .

ONE FACT IS CLEAR: OBEY.
WE KILL, ARE KILLED, ON ALIEN FIELDS
THAT OUR HOMEFIELDS MAY BEAR NO CROPS OF BONES.

CAN LOSERS MEET THEIR FATHER'S EYES?

O LIFT THINE EYES:

OUR FATHER
WHOSE REALM OF LIGHT CONTAINS
THE OCEANS, EARTH AND SKY,
WHO SEES ALL THINGS THEREIN,
SEE AND DELIVER US. . . .

Text

Ast occasus ubi tempusve audere repressit,
Annales, 295

Pila retunduntur venientibus obvia pilis
Ibid., 495

Hic tum nostri cessere parumper.   *Ibid.*, 509

Postquam defessi sunt stare et spargere sese
Ibid., 160

Teneor consipta undique venor.   *Tragoediae*, 305

'Navorum imperium servare est induperantum.
Annales, 405

Dum censent terrere minis, hortantur ibi sos.
Ibid., 244

dictis Romanis incutit iram
Ibid., 460

'Noenu decet mussare bonos qui facta labore
nixi militiae peperere.   *Ibid.*, 434–435

Qui vicit non est victor nisi victus fatetur'
Ibid., 485

'Dum quidem unus homo Romanus toga superescit,
Ibid., 486

'quo res sapsa loco sese ostentatque iubetque.
Ibid., 406

regnumque nostrum ut sospitent
superstitentque.   *Tragoediae*, 299–300

'Quis pater aut cognatus volet vos contra tueri?
Annales, 462

Aspice hoc sublime candens quem invocant omnes Iovem.
Tragoediae, 351

patrem divumque hominumque
Annales, 448

Iuppiter tuque adeo summe qui res omnis inspicis
quique tuo Sol lumine mare terram caelum contines,
inspice hoc facinus priusquam fiat, prohibessis scelus.
Tragoediae, 291–293

IX: THE DUST

High blinding sun.
Looking up, all men cry out O

Day's eye, Seed of light, All-fire, All-father, see us!

I've seen it written that the flesh is dust
but souls are fire taken from the sun.

Sun and moon whose journeys measure earthly dust,
nightrising bestiary of goatstars, crabstars, cupped
how? in the curve between sky's end and earth—

I've felt, shall always feel, an immane reason drives
this family of light. And does not care what passions
drive the family of man. For, if heaven held compassion,
men would take its harmony, and mundane goodness blaze
forever, rage be quenched forever in a raging night—

Absence of care! But I have seen, now see, men dazzled,
squinting heavendeep, snared by spiderthreads of light.
They read light's turning presences, things that are,
for godsigns—things that are to be. Their hearts see
visions that do not accord with sights held in their eyes.
Does no man see what lies before his feet? I have
looked up: Sun rolls in its socket, the colossal sky
curves yellow like an old skull crammed with terrors—

Dustpillars. Sunshafts splintering the molten air.
Vultures soaring, circling on wind's convolutions.
A murder of crows perched in lopped trees.
Before tomorrow's dawn their craws and guts will
grind crude graves for those who lie here fireless,
rusting in their own blood, growing fetid, homing
to first dust: The field's obscene with dust,
the sunshot dust spins heavenhigh, lays waste the sky.
The sun's gone blind. The godfire glitters life
into dead eyes and sits like gold coins on the burnt-out
cores of living eyes that ask enlightenment, O splendor,
horror, godlight bursts from massing javelins, and who
now sees an end to war?
                              A sword, a spear, my naked hands

                              Text

Aspice hoc sublime candens quem invocant omnes Iovem.
                              Tragoediae, 351

                  divumque hominumque pater rex
                              Annales, 449

            Terra corpus est at mentis ignis est
                              Epicharmus, 7

Istic est de sole sumptus ignis
                  isque totus mentis est.
                              Ibid., 8–9

sed sola terrarum postquam permensa parumper,

Annales, 555

astrologorum signa in caelo quid sit observationis,
cum capra aut nepa aut exoritur nomen aliquod beluarum,
quod est ante pedes nemo spectat, caeli scrutantur plagas.

Tragoediae, 249–251

quae cava corpore caeruleo cortina receptat

Varia, 6

Ego deum genus esse semper dixi et dicam caelitum,
sed eos non curare opinor quid agat humanum genus;

Tragoediae, 328–329

nam si curent, bene bonis sit, male malis; quod nunc
    abest.   *Ibid.,* 330

bussus araneae   *Varia,* 28

Lumine sic tremulo terra et cava caerula candent.

Tragoediae, 301

sed mihi ne utiquam cor consentit cum oculorum aspectu.

Ibid., 37

Contemplor
inde loci liquidas pilatasque aetheris oras,

Saturae, 3–4

vix solum complere cohum terroribus caeli.

Annales, 557

avium vulgus
Varia, 27

buxus icta taxus tonsa   *Varia,* 29

Vulturus in silvis miserum mandebat homonem.
Heu! Quam crudeli condebat membra sepulchro!

Annales, 141–142

ferro foedati iacent.

Tragoediae, 168

Terris gentis omnis peperit et resumit denuo;
                                        Epicharmus, 4

              stant pulvere campi   *Annales, 503*

Pulvis fulva volat   *Ibid., 308*

iamque fere pulvis ad caelum vasta videtur
                                        Ibid., 279

Crassa pulvis oritur, omnem pervolat caeli fretum.
                                        Tragoediae, 398

semianimesque micant oculi lucemque requirunt.
                                        Annales, 502

Sparsis hastis longis campus splendet et horret.
                                        Scipio, 6

Quis potis ingentis oras evolvere belli?   *Annales, 173*

Quae mea comminus machaera atque hasta hostibitis manu,
                                        Tragoediae, 192

X: EVENING
        the sun
        wheels quickly down day's western slope

        No longer does despair defeat them;
        now the sun stands at their backs,
        their lengthening shadows stride ahead like heroes.

        Rage excites them,
        the dying day shields them,
        in enemy eyes the setting sun burns pits of night.

        Now iron savagely perceives a chance for victory,
        now combat is embraced,
        man and man coil with their enemies like lovers.

        And do not falter.

Cheers toll in the darkening bell of heaven:
We are as brave as space is limitless!
The battlefield stands witness.

Heatlightning in the cloudless west.
Thunder. Taps.
Or a god's remote laughter.
Stillness.
This onslaught of serenity
intones a benediction: freedom now forever

the evening star

Text

amplius exaugere obstipo lumine solis

Annales, 278

'Non semper vestra evertit; nunc Iuppiter hac stat.'

Ibid., 253

quom soles eadem facient longiscere longe.

Ibid., 438

Inicit inritatus, tenet occasus, iuvat res.

Ibid., 167

Saeviter fortunam ferro cernunt de victoria.

Tragoediae, 193

Viri validis cum viribus luctant.

Annales, 307

spiras legionibus nexit.

Ibid., 498

neque corpora firma
longiscunt quicquam.   *Ibid.,* 436–437

Tollitur in caelum clamor exortus utrimque.

Ibid., 433

Fortes Romani sunt tamquam caelus profundus

Ibid., 470

'Testes sunt Campi Magni. *Scipio,* 14

qui fulmine claro
omnia per sonitus arcet, *Annales, 452–453*

Iuppiter hic risit, tempestatesque serenae
riserunt omnes risu Iovis omnipotentis.
Ibid., 450–451

Tum tonuit laevum bene tempestate serena.
Ibid., 454

'libertatemque, ut perpetuassit
Ibid., 320

Vesper

XI: VICTORY

The heavens whirl, pinpointed with starfires.
Against night's tranquillity glow earth's fires
where carved corpses burn.
The wind, freshening,
fans the sparks; they bloom and spit crisply.

Over the field the victors lie sleepscattered,
all exult, all are safe in the deep cores
of dreams, all healed of battle by the wine
bubbling red through their veins with the most
gentle bitterness.
Like a giant of single
purpose whose belly is stretched and turgid
with human meat, War rests.
A lone flute
made of a shinbone paints tunes on the night.

Text

qui caelum versat stellis fulgentibus aptum.
Annales, 59

Omnes occisi, obcensique in nocte serena.

Ibid., 383

Cum magno strepitu Volcanum ventus vegebat.

Ibid., 531

Omnes mortales victores, cordibus imis
laetantes, vino curatos, somnus repente
in campo passim mollissimus perculit acris.

Ibid., 363–365

Cyclopis venter velut olim turserat alte
carnibus humanis distentus   *Ibid.*, 310–311

Tibia Musarum pangit melos,   *Ibid.*, 291

XII: MIDNIGHT

(eclipse
the
moon
obscured

stars
wash
strewn
earth
and
dusty
mourning
dark
like
women's
tears)

Text

—nonis Iunis soli luna obstitit et nox   *Annales,* 166

strata terrae lavere lacrumis vestem squalam et sordidam
                                                Tragoediae, 323

EPITAPH

Look, young poets, on the deathmask of an old poet
who painted for your inner eyes the deeds and deaths
        of great men.
Cry no tears, let no funerals of salt erode the cold
        stone face.
Life is poems soaring bloodwarm from living tongues.

Text

Aspicite o cives senis Enni imaginis formam.
        Hic vestrum pinxit maxima facta patrum.
Nemo me lacrimis decoret nec funera fletu
        faxit. Cur? Volito vivus per ora virum.

THE VOICE OF CLAUDIA

ANONYMOUS EPITAPH

ABOUT 150 B.C.

Worldguest, stand, listen, let the stone speak.
It is the small graved unbeautiful voice of a
woman once beautiful.
The name her parents named her is
Claudia.
She loved her husband with a thankful love
and bore him two sons: of these two, one
she left on earth, one she lost to earth.
With gentle words, with perfect dignity
she armored her house. She spun a lifethread.
It is said.
Go.

Text

Hospes, quod deico paullum est; asta ac pellege.
Heic est sepulcrum hau pulcrum pulcrai feminae.
Nomen parentes nominarunt Claudiam.
Suom mareitom corde deilexit souo.
Gnatos duos creavit, horunc alterum
in terra linquit, alium sub terra locat.
Sermone lepido, tum autem incessu commodo.
Domum servavit, lanam fecit. Dixi. Abei.

Tituli Sepulcrales, 18

POSSIBILITIES

THE BELLE OF THE BALL

Well, she thinks she's the
whole ballgame, bouncebounce, an allaround girl for all men:
toss a nod, bat a lash, volley lovelooks, catch, caress,
catch underhand, under table call the signals with a toe,
spin a sportsfan through the hoop, throw an intercepted kiss—
when one man cheers, she fakes a pass at someone else.

—after Naevius

Text

Quasi pila
in choro ludens datatim dat se et communem facit.
Alii adnutat, alii adnictat, alium amat alium tenet.
Alibi manus est occupata, alii pervellit pedem;
anulum dat alii spectandum, a labris alium invocat,
cum alio cantat, at tamen alii suo dat digito litteras.
Fabulae palliatae, 74–79

LUCILIUS
180?–102? B.C.
ARS SATYRICA

† quod is † intellegebar posse † haud † ad paucos rettuli.

735

Because I am understood to possess a poet's powers,
a few friends have said, WRITE . . .

IN THE BEGINNING, SO THOSE WHO STUDY NATURE SAY,
THERE WAS SPIRIT AND THERE WAS CLAY.

. . . ON NATURAL HISTORY

1.

Fire, air, earth, and water

Muses, help me, I'd genuinely like to please my friends,

to quest the genesis storm, the elemental time
when heaven and earth were created,
the land cradled unformed in nightmists and downpour;
and tell of volcanoes first breasting the torrents
to stand firm, eternal, come winds, come wild water,
and igniting the darkness—fireshowers! celebrations!
That godstruck world quaked and rang
hit by hammering thunder

Afterwards,
sunrise, dew . . .

a gentleness . . .
something holy
dwelling in the
day's warmth, breezes, fertile earth, and ocean salt
But—

Text

Principio physici omnes constare hominem ex anima et
    corpore
dicunt.   676–677

                               Prodes amicis. 1187

"Vellem cumprimis, fieri si forte potisset, . . .

                                  19

Aetheris et terrae genitabile quaerere tempus.

                                  1

Terra abit in nimbos umoremque.   615

Tanti se e tenebris montes eis aetera tollent.

                                 848

fluctibus a ventisque adversis firmiter essent.

                                 420

crebrae ut scintillae, in stricturis quod genus olim
ferventi ferro.   146–147

Et velut in fabrica fervens cum marculus ferrum
⟨mugitu⟩ multo cum magnis ictibus tundit,   1265–1266

Suda . . .   . . . remillum 621

            Serena caeli numina et salsi fretus.
                                884

. . . ON NATURAL HISTORY

2.
—we've all heard this natural history before.
It's been immortalized in a dozen versions,
some nearly as ancient as that era.
Why reiterate their famous visions?
And why not? Pick a phrase here, a
passage there—mmm easy, tempting,

and a fraud, a ripe skin round a core of fakery.
To rearrange old truths and call them new,
preempt old tales for a song and vend illusion—
feckless ingenuity for genius—and plume oneself on
mastermending, expert crazy quilting—ridiculous!
There's firstrate work for lunatics and mortal fools.

Yes, I'm afraid of being so accused.
Old times have given me other than old poems to muse

moon that paints the moonscales of the riverfishes silver,
sun that warms the green grapes to a royal purple,
wine that tastes as if it's full of sungold,
fields and hills to ride a good horse over,
breath for singing songs in my own manner

and—

I envy nobody, no, not I.
Not often.

Text

Fandam atque auditam iterabimus famam. 53

archeotera . . . unde haec sunt omnia nata.
411

Est illud quoque mite malum, blandum atque dolosum.
1003

Plure foras vendunt quod † pro minore emptum †
1160

ut perhibetur iners ars in quo non erit ulla.
474

"In re agenda, ipsa ridicula iactat se†deret †"

840

"sarcinatorem esse summum, suere centonem optume."

841

te primum cum istis, insanum hominem et cerebrosum.

519

Habes omnem rem; timeo ne accuser.   813

Non numquam dabit ipsa aetas quod possit habendo.

1058

Luna alit ostrea et implet echinos, muribus fibras
et iecur addit.   1222–1223

purpureamque uvam facit albam pampinum habere.

1224

defusum e pleno χρυσίζον . . . vinum,   1226

qui campos collesque gradu perlabitur uno,   506

                    bonum schema   416

nulli me invidere, non strabonem fieri saepius
deliciis me istorum.   766–767

. . . ON NATURAL HISTORY

3.
    —a principle for wooing Muses:
Let creation's end be consonant with its beginning;
inspired first lines deserve like afterwords.
And, glory of glories, the world's first dawn?

                    Suppose

I'd like to find words capturing the spirit of ances-
        tral poets,

catching the attention of my people, too, making eyes
blink as the dazzle of the world's first sunlight
bursts newminted, splendid in their minds—

I couldn't do it.

These days each day forcing sliverlight, come winter,
        come hot weather,
through night's niggardly fissures turns out to be
one more Friday the thirteenth. Reality
clips fancy's flight. Insight, outsight, indivisible.

My images

are generated by the odious sights, the common stenches
conquering my senses—

Text

                    Principio exitus dignus
exodiumque sequatur.   414–415

Sume diem qui est visus tibi pulcherrimus unus.

                                                585

Nunc itidem populo . . . his cum scriptoribus;
voluimus capere animum illorum.   720–721

[praestringat oculorum aciem] splendore micanti.

                                                1004

ut si id quod concupisset non aptus foret,   862

            Dic quaenam cogat vis ire minutim
per commissuras rimarum noctis nigrore.   247–248

                "anno vertenti dies
tetri miseri ac religiosi."   838–839

"Eidola atque atomus vincere Epicuri volam." 820

                    quaeque aspectu sunt spurca et odore.

                                                851

There staggers Quint the True Blue Blood, once famous for
his body's beauty (though infamous for beauty's deeds),
who seemed our most munificent companion & the macho-
est of men, who could outeat outdrink outspend outstud
outsin us every one & thought he'd so perform indefinitely
without incurring any penalty account he was a rich
man's son. He's drained his liquid assets to the dregs, our
liking too, yet pays & pays a present price for exploits
past that no one dares repeat & all he strives for slithers
out of reach. He's senile now, an ugly undernourished
stiff, limply lickerish & liverish, gas bellies him, bile makes
him gag. One pleasure has remained in this adversity—
his cups, but one more drink's enough to lay his dust for-
ever in the dust.

Here shuffles Lamia that Canny Belle, once graceful lithe light-
hearted slenderbodied as a boy (though boyish not at all
indeed), who in one year—what year?—disembowled dis-
cuppered deglassed desilvered deplated completely de-
pleted her husband then decamped to vamp The Blood.
Licking his lips her lips with love she tendered him &
sharptoothed soft-tongued in one clean swoop devotedly
devoured him, substance spirit, whole. She gums now
shivers starves excruciatingly, the squalidest & scabbiest
of sluts whom those who never loved her envy not &
those who loved her once no longer want, unfragrant she
unlaved unlusted for & never to be laid by man again.

Pause. Observe a moment, dirtspotted dress meets dungstained
robe, no shame in either one. O she bloodies him with
her hysteric curses, he's turning red & uncurbed fires his
body's Latin back at her, she's flushed.

Dropjawed we can't help snickering, our grins are rictuses.

For—

Quintus Opimius ille, Iugurtini pater huius,
et formosus homo fuit et famosus, utrumque
primo adulescens; posterius dat rectius sese.

450–452

Munifici comesque amicis nostris videamur viri.

657

quandoquidem reperti magnis conbibonum ex copiis . . .

658

      "Peccare impune rati sunt
posse et nobilitate facul propellere iniquos."

270–271

Vertitur oenophori fundus, sententia nobis.   132

Tantalus qui poenas, ob facta nefantia, poenas
pendit.   136–137

quod deformis senex ἀρθριτικὸs ac podagrosus
est, quod mancus miserque exilis ramite magno.

354–355

Anxit quem febris una atque una ἀπεψία,
vini inquam cyathus unus potuit tollere.   976–977

Id solum adversae fortunae reque resistit.   266

"Illo quid fiat Lamia et Bitto oxyodontes
quod veniunt, illae gumiae evetulae improbae ineptae?"

1028–1029

      quod gracila est, pernix, quod pectore puro,
quod puero similis.   324–325

"utrum anno an horno tete abstuleris a viro."

794

"depoclassere aliqua sperans me ac deargentassere
decalauticare, eburno speculo despeculassere."

640–641

Praeservit, labra delingit, delenit amore.   1106

"Quam non solum devorare se omnia ac devorrere"
                                                    740

                    Hic cruciatur fame
frigore inluvie inbalnitie inperfunditie incuria.
                                                    727–728

squalitate summa ac scabie summa in aerumna obrutam,
neque inimicis invidiosam, neque amico exoptabilem.
                                                    729–730

Quod si paulisper captare atque observare haec volueris,
                                                    769

Hanc vestimentis maculosis tu aspice, siste.   1040

              quandoque pudor ex pectore cessit,
                                                    1046

Haec inbubinat at contra te inbulbitat ⟨ille⟩.
                                                    1182

Malas tollimus nos atque utimur . . . rictu.   131

              . . . ON NATURAL HISTORY

4.

          —manscapes present I-lands   incontinents
            old young peakèd face lowlying tongue
      gulley gullet gorgebelly humpback heart of stone
        knockknee bandyshank straightfoot splayfoot
         wart scar bubo ulcer pustulous eruption—
            there are differences in the insignia
                but each skull is supported by
                          a neck
                      each pelvis by
                       two thighs
                       each man

is mothered in a bag of waters and outpoured to light to breath
and every man stirs up his pisspot tempests
that excite unholy admiration for a month a day
but never forever.

And all men live it up a little, live down a lot, live out
their numbered months
and the passing time will bring each one the finest final
cure for life

and lead him home into the great grave sept
where he shall meet his bride his Death.

He brings no portion with him, keeps nothing, leaves nothing.
And no man's
honored long, long wept for, long remembered.
For in these times our times everything men do men are

burns out blows down turns into dust is sucked back in the
worldpool of the spinning years.

What—

Text

Perminxi lectum, inposui † pedem † pellibus labes.

1183

baro)num ac rupicum squarr(osa incondita) rostra

1184

atque omnes mandonum gulae.   988

et ventrem et gutturem eundem.

1233

gibbere magno.   1213

insignis varis cruribus et petilis.

628

Nasum rectius nunc homini est suraene pedesne?

627

inguen ne existat, papulae, tama, ne boa noxit.

1246

Tamen aut verruca aut cicatrix melius; papulae differunt.

743

Caput
collo sustentatur, truncus autem coxendicibus.

997–998

ita uti quisque nostrum e bulga est matris in lucem editus.

704

'Non peperit, verum postica parte profudit.'   111

            "ut multos mensesque diesque,
non tamen aetatem, tempestatem hanc scelerosi
mirentur."   39–41

qui sex menses vitam ducunt, Orco spondent septimum.

659

aetatem istuc tibi laturam, et bellum si hoc bellum putas.

971

hoc invenisse unum ad morbum illum, homini vel bellissimum.

969

Cum sciam nihil esse in vita proprium mortali datum,

777

nullo honore, heredis fletu nullo, nullo funere.

790

Intereunt labuntur eunt rursum omnia vorsum.   1188

. . . ON NATURAL HISTORY

5.

    —can we give to future generations?

    For substance and shape, with wordplays and down-to-
        earth verses,

I have courted the Muses.

                              They have said,
Lucilius, what impels you to importune us?

      —Once on a Greek height the winged horse was
           bridled.
       Now let me gentle you, let me ride—

O Muses unmounted, hotblooded Muses, they're skittish
    as virgins
and do not easily yield to a man.

                              They have said,
If we dare give ourselves, how will you use us?

How quicken us who hold now and ever all songs worth
    the singing?
You revel in rage, your hand would abuse us.
Break us! Yoke us! No, we are not willing

to cultivate dirt. We cannot accept your lewdness
and sermons.

                 And they have said,
Be content, hoarse man, with your own amusements.

Flaring redhot, roaring, digging up an earthy verb,
    spitting bitter salty words,

                all right—

Text

Cuius vultu ac facie ludo ac sermonibus nostris
virginis hoc pretium atque hunc reddebamus honorem.

                             1039–1040

"Verum tu quid agis? Interpella me, ut sciam."

                       819

    "Ante ego te vacuam atque animosam
Tessalam ut indomitam frenis subigamque domemque."

                          1041–1042

At non sunt similes neque dant. Quid si dare vellent?
Acciperesne? Doce.   921–922

"Quid mihi proderit quam satias iam omnium rerum tenet?"
                                                        964

                        Tu qui iram indulges nimis
manus a muliere abstinere melius est.   855–856

"Tune iugo iungas me autem et succedere aratro
invitam et glebas subigas proscindere ferro?"

                                                     1043–1044

ravi

et te his versibus interea contentus teneto.   1015

                    Ore salem expiravit amarum.

                                                        1262

. . . ON NATURAL HISTORY

6.

—I'm in my element.

I go where the present facts of living lead
and do whatever past experience deems meet,
though visions still seduce and hope occasionally
        seizes me,
the side-tracked poet greedy for some kind of pro-
        geny.

And in these mean times I embrace the Zeitgeist,
and if I give her what she cries for, let her ride—
she'll turn the trick, she'll be my muse, my night-
screwed bitch, and mother-midwife to my lines.

        What does she cry for? Songs to sting
        the stolid citizens! Hearthitting punchlines!
        Ring, room! Reverberate, you rafters, echoing
        the hundred hundred solecisms engendered by

our words & ways! I'll extemporize a new un-
    natural
history, I'll eff the ineffable

                              Fevers,
                    cerebrations . . .
manstruck, I have headaches hammering my temples
after words

Friends, help me, I'd like to please the genuine Muses.

                    Text

aut quod animum induxit semel et utile omnino putat.
                                        775

Illo oculi deducunt ipsi atque animum spes illuc rapit.
                                        776

"qua propter deliro et cupidi officium fungor liberum."
                                        646

iam qua tempestate vivo chresin ad me recipio.
                                        778

Si vero das quod rogat et si suggeris suppus,

                                        926

carissam

noctipugam ⟨medica⟩   1179

            Quid quaerimus? Acri
inductum cantu stolidum . . .   1127–1128
cordipugis versibus

            Resultabant aedesque lacusque.
                                        1236

Adde soloecismon genera atque vocabula centum.
                                        397

. . . dissociata aeque omnia ac nefantia. 886

Querquera consequitur . . . capitisque dolores.

196

LUCILIUS, PLEASE ENTERTAIN US, FEAST US ON THE FRUITS
OF YOUR IMAGINATION, SING . . .

. . . ABOUT MIRACULOUS SIGHTS
AND EXOTIC ANIMALS

Sea serpent, hippogriff, snake with feathered wings—
I've never seen one of these things.

But I have seen
    —a man flounder and land in the soup
    a slave make a monkey out of his master
    the master make an ass of himself—
                    manimals.

And I have seen
    —an old woman turn to a winebottle—
                    miracle.

Traveling south to the Strait of Messina,
I met a girl like a threshing machine. A
    flail of her loins
    & she harvested coins
from leering old lecher and young libertine. AAAAHHH,

LUCILIUS, THAT'S TERRIBLE!

Text

pulchre invitati acceptique benigne.

595

"miracla † ciet † elephantas.
                              17

camphippi elephantocamelos

nisi portenta anguisque volucris ac pinnatos scribitis.
                                                    723

Occidunt, Lupe, saperdae te et iura siluri!   46
                              vernam ac cercupithecon.
                                             1214

    uti pecudem te asinumque ut denique nasci
praestiterit.   1129–1130

                "Hinc ad me hinc, licet;
'anus russum ad armillum.' "   831–832

hunc molere, illam autem ut frumentum vannere lumbis,
                                             302

Crisabit ut si frumentum clunibus vannat.   361

CONCOCT A SPICY SERMON, A REAL SIZZLER, AD LIB.

From dawn till late at night, weekdays and Sundays, too,
the have-nots and the haves alike and all at once swarm
in the downtown streets and squares and don't go home
but, one and all, devote themselves to the same old games—
mouthing promises with fingers crossed and rigging odds,
smoothing conflicts with cajolery, aping—making apes of—
    decent men and
setting snares of lies as if each one were enemy to every
    other:

To be a man is having power to pay in full the fitting
    price
for the events we bring upon ourselves and those life
    brings to us;
to be a man is knowing what effect on man events may
    have;

to be a man, to know what's right for man, and useful,
    honor-brightening—
the good, the bad as well—what's useless, twisting,
    honor-blackening;
to be a man, to know why truth is to be sought, and how
    to seek it;
to be a man, to pay truth's price from self-earned
    means;
to be a man, to give each man his due according to his
    deeds:
be stranger and forever enemy to evil men and vile pur-
    suits,
stand against them as defender of good men and godly
    ways,
and magnify these men, wish these men well, and live
    with them in amity;
to be a man, to pledge one's loyalty above all else to
    native land,
and then to family, and last and least to self.

Text

"bene cocto et
condito, sermone bono et, si quaeris, libenter."

206–207

Nunc vero a mani ad noctem festo atque profesto
totus item pariterque die populusque patresque
iactare indu foro se omnes, decedere nusquam;
uni se atque eidem studio omnes dedere et arti—
verba dare ut caute possint, pugnare dolose,
blanditia certare, bonum simulare virum se,
insidias facere ut si hostes sint omnibus omnes.

1145–1151

Virtus, Albine, est pretium persolvere verum
quis in versamur quis vivimus rebus potesse;
virtus est homini scire id quod quaeque habeat res;

virtus scire homini rectum utile quid sit honestum,
quae bona quae mala item, quid inutile turpe inhonestum;
virtus quaerendae finem re scire modumque;
virtus divitiis pretium persolvere posse;
virtus id dare quod re ipsa debetur honori,
hostem esse atque inimicum hominum morumque malorum
contra defensorem hominum morumque bonorum,
hos magni facere, his bene velle, his vivere amicum,
commoda praeterea patriai prima putare,
deinde parentum, tertia iam postremaque nostra.

1196–1208

LUCILIUS, YOU MAKE A SOUR AND SORRY PREACHER. TELL
US OF <u>WOMEN,</u> AND HOW THEY HAVE ENSLAVED US WITH THEIR
CHARMS.

MADAM X

What she is I know full well—
a bawd of disarming deceit.
Who she is I will not tell—
her name doesn't fit in these feet.

DEFLOWER POWER

Clematis, no bowered virgin she. Nor meant to be.
Yet does she seem made new, inviolate,
whenever love employs us in its ultimate embrace:
only he who tears the rapture from her rosy face
may claim to have deflowered her.

one fruit to pick in snowy weather: cherries

"Adde eodem, tristis ac severus philosophus."

821

Hymnis cantando quae me adseruisse ait ad se,

1168

aetatem et faciem ut saga et bona conciliatrix.

291

Servorum est festus dies hic
quem plane hexametro versu non dicere possis.

252–253

Hymnis sine eugio † ac destina † .   896

"lustratus, piatus."

76

"Tum latus conponit lateri et cum pectore pectus."

333

et Hymnidis ac si
ex facie florem delegeris.   1166–1167

Hiemem unamquamque carpam.   878

LUCILIUS, ENOUGH OF YOUR CRANKY AMOURS! GIVE US, IF
IT'S NOT AN IRKSOME TASK, A FEW JUDICIOUS WORDS ON
WORDS—WHICH ONES TO CHOOSE AND HOW THEY'RE USED.

. . . ON VERBS

The Inseparable Adjunct

To drink. Give me a cup.
It's not important if I
drink the contents *down* or *up.*

The Split Infinitive

to difFER
to di vide
to d i s s i p a t e
  distress
to distress
  distress

Text

Lucili, si in amore inritarit suo.   814

"Sed tamen hoc dicas quid sit, si noenu molestum est."
                1118

Horum est iudicium, crisis ut describimus ante;
hoc est, quid sumam quid non, in quoque locemus.
             417–418

'abbibere'; hic non multum est 'd' siet an 'b.'
             393

"dividant differant dissipent distrahant."   909

YOU <u>ARE</u> AN EDUCATED MAN, A MAN OF LETTERS—AREN'T YOU?

. . . A LETTER
to Sardinia

My dear dear dearest friend,
        I send this salvo
of salutes to wish you nothing but the best
of health. I'd like to think you think of me
as your dear friend and have so favored me
since friendship ripened in our halfripe manhoods
when we tried and proved each other, mind and body,
to the hilt. Together we let off steam sprinting

around the track, wrestling in the gym, swotting
Homer. Together we bloated ourselves drunk
on warm beer . . . loitered, horny as two Ethiopian
rhinos, at the hopeless stagedoor of the local
skinshow . . . sowed our oats another year in the same
plowed furrow (or were our wallets reaped?) . . . and
bleated hymns next morning in the crowded church.
We shared joys and praises, suffered their reverse.
And you and I, we roamed the fields of greening life
like lioncubs young and wild in pride, delighting
equally in everything and quick to believe
delight would last forever.
                          We're older now.
Not everything is forever possible, although your
world still truckles to your luck and golden looks.
I don't. Therefore you call me 'reprobate.' Have it
your way. For, to your heart's vast desires I am
wholeheartedly averse. From your body's prime
cupidities, my reason shies. You've strived your
utmost to mount certain heights, and, utterly
dissimilar to you, I till my bottomlands and write
when the least inspiration strikes. And, as you say,
your secrets, meant for safe deposit in my ears alone,
have slithered to my murmurous tongue, my pen
has published private mysteries for every passerby.
What would you have me do? Keep silent?
(And let you then suggest that I'm uneducated?
Worse. Illiterate?) Or should I lie about a good
old friend? I have bad habits, yes. Libel
isn't one of them.
                   I am your faithful loving
friend. As fortunemaking binds your fortuneteller
to your lucky stars, so friendship binds me
to the mundane truth. I've told the truth about
your diverse deals and profitless percentages . . .
the gluttony that feasts upon the vitals of your
honesty . . . the debts you owe for three-ring binges

banging tawdry broads . . . rump sessions wrestling
with clean-shaven queens, rebarbative performances
with the members of the ballet corps. You know
I know you better than *you* know you. I know
you are both maculate and vincible, a barely
breathing man, a shadow version of your lionself.
And I know, too, you'll ask why I would drag you
from your deeds and destinations, and what
they have to do with me.

                       I help my friends.
I'll try to sum it up for you. You are well-
versed in vice. And I am shamelessly vice
versa; my only license is poetic. For me, a mortal
heap of blood and bones, a muse has spread immortal
gates. And guided me within. And I have come
to show you yourself, a sick and played-out lion,
sad, corrupted, scabrous, and plainly your dander's
down. I must speak out (a poet silenced is as good
as dead) and put in verses the advices I must give:

    Hellraising like yours—
        peckish scrabbles after coins,
            entrapment by a tenderloin,
                slitting the hairy purses of whores:
    it's not for these we undertake to live our
            dwindling hours.

    Prefer to be called poor
        but upright in the end
            by a few living friends
                than let Hell raise you as its lord—
    la goule régnante de millions d'âmes et
            de corps morts.

                    My dearest friend,
I savage you with salutations to wish you nothing
but salvation.

Depend on me, I shall remain
your most perversely speechful friend,

Lucilius
in Sicily

To cry and preconfess premeditated sin
and ask the pardon of the gods
before you hump some hooker is
to rite a wrong

Text

Quidni? Et tu idem inlitteratum me atque idiotam diceres.

674

"Salvere iubere salutem est mittere amico."   261

Favitorem tibi me, amicum, amatorem putes,   874

tuam probatam mi et spectatam maxume adulescentiam.

689

"Cum stadio in gymnasio in duplici corpus siccassem pila,"

688

obtursi ebrius.   164

". . . 'stulte saltatum te inter venisse cinaedos.'

33

rinocerus velut Aethiopus   184

hunc molere, illam autem ut frumentum vannere lumbis.

302

aut operatum aliquo in celebri cum aequalibus fano.

1098

Tu partem laudis caperes, tu gaudia mecum
partisses.   94–95

concursaret agros, catulos fetumque ferai. . . .   155

                        Aeque fruniscor ego ac tu.   583

Fuimus pernices, aeternum id nobis sperantes fore.
                                                783

'Maior erat natu; non omnia possumus omnes.'   246

Omnes formonsi, fortes tibi, ego inprobus; esto.
                                        1077

et quod tibi magno opere cordi est, mihi vehementer
    displicet,   701

ut ego effugiam quod te in primis cupere apisci intellego.
                                        702

summis nitere opibus, at ego contra ut dissimilis siem.
                                        703

Si messes facis et Musas si vendis Lavernae,   564

At enim dicis "clandestino tibi quod conmisum foret,
neu muttires quidquam neu mysteria ecferres foras."
                                    672–3

". . . quid ipsum me facere optes."   264

Homini amico et familiari non est mentiri meum.
                                        695

Nolito tibi me male dicere posse putare,   1069

Porro amici est bene praecipere, Tusci bene praedicere.
                                        694

verum et mercaturae omnes et quaesticuli isti
intuti . . .   341–342

quod sumptum atque epulas victu praeponis honesto.
                                        1234

quem sumptum facis in lustris circum oppida lustrans.

1071

"Podicis, Hortensi, est ad eam rem nata palaestra."

1180

inberbi androgyni, barbati moechocinaedi.   1048

quem scis scire tuas omnes maculasque notasque.

1070

"vix vivo homini ac monogrammo.'

56

Quid servas quo eam quid agam? Quid id attinet ad te?

1083

Prodes amicis.   1187

Summatim tamen experiar rescribere paucis.   1063

Sublatus pudor omnis, licentia fenus refertur.

1047

cui sua committunt mortali claustra Camenae.   1064

Producunt me ad te, tibi me haec ostendere cogunt.   1065
                              leonem

aegrotum et lassum   1111–1112

tristem et corruptum scabie et porriginis plenum.

1115

si liceat facere et iam hoc versibus reddere quod do.

1066

Mihi necesse est eloqui,
nam scio Amyclas tacendo periise.   696–697

at qui nummos tristis inuncat.

530

Illi praeciso atque epulis capiuntur opimis.   604

"in bulgam penetrare pilosam.

                                                    61

scorta   Pyrgensia.   1178

Non idcirco extollitur nec vitae vegrandi datur.

                                                    705

non paucis malle ac sapientibus esse probatum
ἦ πᾶσιν νεκύεσσι καταφθιμένοισιν ἀνάσσειν.   491–492

                    e Sicula Lucilius Sardiniensem
terram.   287–288

⟨Absterge lacrimas⟩ et divos ture precemur
consilium fassi, placeatne impune luperis.   249–250

NOT EPISTLES, LUCILIUS. LETTERS!

. . . THE ALPHABET

A is first and there I'll begin.
When the others are named
my song will end.

Great A, little a, bouncing B,
the cook's peeling onions
and weeping copiously.

FOR THE MAN WHO
PUTS WORDS IN MY MOUTH

You don't yet know what it is that I don't know.
Yet, my question quarter-asked, you answer me.
How? Q & A through ESP.

Text

'a' primum est, hinc incipiam, et quae nomina ab hoc
  sunt. . . .
'aa' primum longa, 'a' brevis syllaba; . . .   368–369

flebile cepe simul lacrimosaeque ordine tallae.

                                                    216

"Si me nescire hoc nescis quod quaerere dico,
quare divinas quicquam? an tu quaerere debes
ipse? et si scis q. b. e. scire hoc d. t."   30–32

R

The letter R . . . a cur enraged snarls it
more clearly than a man can.

You, whom I once honored as a fair man,
took sudden joy in cutting me with slander.
You gutted, plucked and stuffed me,
lambasted me with ridicule: because your verses
lay like wormfood on neglected shelves,
you publicly recited mine in a ruinous rasp.

And got away with it. I rushed at you
courageously, calling you a rotmouthed wretch,
a robber, a wrinkled rhinoceros. Now
that your poems again are read with mine,
you ask me to apologize. I won't.
I made no error when I growled at you

in doggish. It's not my fault
that R errs in its own name.

Text

                    ⟨r littera . . .⟩
inritata canes quam homo quam planius dicit. 3–4
sicuti te quem aequae speciem vitae esse putamus.

                                    1074

POSSIBILITIES   151

Gaudes cum de me ista foris sermonibus differs.

1085

et maledicendo in multis sermonibus differs. 1086

Quin totum purges devellas me atque deuras
exultes ⟨adequites⟩ et sollicites. 1088–1089

et sua perciperet retro rellicta iacere, 1090

rassuro tragicus qui carmina perdit Oreste 594

            Inde canino ricto oculisque
involem. 1000–1001

        ore
corupto 1255

Homo inpuratus et inpuno est rapinator. 57

rinocerus velut Aethiopus 184

et sola ex multis nunc nostra poemata ferri 1091

'r'; non multum est hoc cacosyntheton atque canina
si lingua dico; nihil ad me; nomen enim illi est.

389–390

S

Monstrificabile
Marcus Pacuvius,
translating Sophocles,
seldom wrote S.

Hellenophilia
dictated Σ. We
hear actors speak half-essed
words nonetheless.

It's not a little or a light job to teach mud the ABC's.

Text

. . . Nunc ignobilitas his mirum ac monstrificabile.

726

's' nostrum et semigraeci quod dicimus 'sigma'
nil erroris habet.   391–392

"nihil parvi ac pensi, uti litteras doceas lutum."

826

TRY <u>YOUR</u> HAND AT TRAGEDY.

> (Enter hardships and hard work, exit Lucilius.
> I'd like to leave quickly without an argument.
> Anybody seen a *deus ex machina*?)

YOU'RE ATTEMPTING TO EVADE US. DON'T PUSSYFOOT.

> Then listen, learn . . .

. . . OF TRUE TRAGEDIES

Now do you seriously think

that any of those oldtime sadtime girls did not clothe
a host of flaws between artfully turned ankles
and artificial curls?

that their breasts unharnessed never did dangle as far
down as belly or, occasionally, the pubic triangle?

or that Alcmena bedded by Zeus (who disguised himself
not as bull, rain of gold, or randy swan but as
her lawfully wedded spouse Amphitryon

in order to facilitate the fathering of Hercules)—do
you think she couldn't have had knockknees or
shanks like an empty pair of parentheses?

and that others, even *la petite parisienne* Helen, who—
I'd rather not say it; the proper impropriety is
up to you—

that such a lass, born to a fine family, brought up in
   a palace, could never have sprouted warts, moles,
   pimples, or one simple callus?

and that other toothsome tragiqueens never cracked smiles
   merely because of relentlessly rotten luck? or were
   their upper incisors noticeably buck?

Achilles was a heel and Agamemnon no game man.

Text

ne hoc faciat atque ex hac is aerumna exeat.   812

nil ut discrepet ac τὸν δ'ἐξήρπαξεν 'Απόλλων
fiat.   267–268

Sed fuga fingitur; ut timido pede percitus vadit!
                                                   845

praeterea ut nostris animos adtendere dictis
atque adhibere velis.   910–911

"Num censes calliplocamon callisphyron ullam
non licitum esse uterum atque etiam inguina tangere
      mammis,
conpernem aut varam fuisse Amphitryonis acoetin
Alcmenam atque alias, Helenam ipsam denique—nolo
dicere; tute vide atque disyllabon elige quodvis—
κούρην eupatereiam aliquam rem insignem habuisse,
verrucam naevum punctum dentem eminulum unum?"
                                                   567–573

Ego enim contemnificus fieri et fastidire Agamemnonis.
                                                   666

HYBRISTIC MADNESS! MAY THE GODS GRANT FORGIVENESS.
IT'S TIME FOR YOU TO TURN YOUR MIND TO WHOLLY SERIOUS
AND USEFUL LINES. TELL US OF BATTLES AND VIRTUOUS
MEN, HOW EXTREME THEIR ADVERSITIES AND HOW STAUNCHLY
OVERCOME, WITH WORDS THAT HONOR BOTH YOUR TALENT AND
THE PRISTINE PAGE AND BUILD ENDURING MONUMENTS TO
INTESTINAL FORTITUDE.

. . . ON GUTS

Quickery quackery
Quintus Opimius,
straining his bowels in
utter despair,

hourly swallowed non-
pharmacological
potions. But that was a
piddling affair.

Text

"Di monerint meliora, amentiam averruncassint tuam!"
665

aut quod animum induxit semel et utile omnino putat.
775

Ut semel in Caeli pugnas te invadere vidi,   1008

quantas quoque modo aerumnas quantosque labores
exanclaris.   1011–1012
et virtute tua, et claris conducere cartis.   1013

Haec virtutis tuae cartis monumenta locantur.

1014

ut si eluviem facere per ventrem velis,
cura ne omnibus distento corpore expiret viis.

684–685

pulmentaria ut intibus aut aliqua id genus herba
et ius maenarum, bene habet; sed mictilis haec est.

1032–1033

NO! COMPOSE A PANEGYRIC ON POMPILIUS'S CAMPAIGN, CITE
CORNELIUS'S ACCCOMPLISHMENTS IN SONG!

> Sing a jingle on a losing general, pander to the com-
> mander who replaces him. Let someone else nurse cos-
> tive men at personal expense. Let someone else defraud
> his genius through tolerance.

. . . OF HISTORY

Seduced by what he's read in books, my young acquaintance
scribbles metered ancient history. He's asked me
for advice and technical assistance.
And I've asked him
how past events can save a present population.

When people read my lines they'll understand
that wisdom comes from traveling always toward good ends
although the road be difficult and dirty.
In other words
he thinks wholeheartedly that history can teach us lessons.

Ah yes, through history I come to share with you a common
interest in a common past and thus we find a common bond
with other men.
I'll drink to that one.
In common, so doctors say, we all begin as animated mud.

Oh no, we learn that though we've fallen to superior force
and often lost our skirmishes, we've never known the horrors
of complete defeat by enemies, we've always won our wars:
therein lies all we need to know.
I quickly issue
caveats and urge him to avoid such arrogance.

And tell him all I know is, every man's his own adeptest
enemy in a damn hard war, and every young man trips
toward dotage, and the road betrays his every step
with pitfall or pratfall, and—
                    From a lover of wisdom
that's a disagreeable and negative opinion.

—and he shares with me as much as men have ever
held in common, matter, mind. One sick, both suffer.
How hold the two together now? Harvests fail, welfare
rolls and bellies bloat, dregs and bitter herbs are
sweet: let common men eat pride and shit, there's
nothing else.
                    Dear god! preserve me from this filth.
His head is filled with rot and worms, he will not listen,

but tranquilly transfers himself from living tumult
to dead calms, and there, in peace, he plays at
wargames: the navies battle, bobbling like tubbed boats
on his hexameters, the kings and captains foot it
toward the wars whose outcomes have been set
by anciently cast bones. He's having fun but is no smarter.
Advice runs off his brain like water.
                    Well the hell
with the breaker of bookspines! Lord, save the poet.

Text

Percrepa pugnam Popili, facta Corneli cane.   714

Curet aegrotum, sumtum homini praebeat, genium suum
defrudet, ali parcat.   692–693

Veterem historiam, inductus studio, scribis ad amores tuos;
                                                           700

ut nunc in hac re mihi opem atque auxilium offeras.
                                                           872

quo populum atque urbem pacto servare potisset
amplius Romanam.   6–7

Sin autem hoc vident, bona semper petere sapientem [et]
putant,   706

Praeterea omne iter est hoc labosum atque lutosum.

98

Tibi porro istaec res idcirco est cordi quod rere utilem.

707

. . . quam mihi quantum est inter humanum genus
rerumque inter se coniugat communicat!   870–871

Assensus sum homini.   464

Principio physici omnes constare hominem ex anima et
corpore
dicunt.   676–677

ut Romanus populus victus vei, superatus proeliis
saepe est multis, bello vero numquam, in quo sunt omnia.

708–709

contra flagitium nescire bello vinci a barbaro
Viriato, Annibale.   710–711

quid cavendum tibi censerem, quid vitandum maxume.

712

et saevo ac duro in bello multo optimus hostis.

1124

"Prospiciendum ergo in senectam iam nunc adulescentiaest."

837

"Adde eodem, tristis ac severus philosophus."

821

Animo qui aegrotat videmus corpore hunc signum dare;

678

tum doloribus confectum corpus animo obsistere.

679

Deficit alma Ceres, nec plebes pane potitur,   214

"rugosum atque fami plenum."   460

                        nam mel regionibus illis
incrustatus calix rutai caulis habetur.   128–129

Deum rex avertat verba obscena!   858

"ne auriculam obsidat caries, ne vermiculi qui."

                                                                  298

quodque te in tranquillum ex saevis transfers tempestatibus.
                                                                  717

Naumachiam licet haec inquam alveolumque putare et
calces; delectes te, hilo non rectius vivas.   489–490

Haec tu si voles per auris pectus inrigarier,

                                                                  690

"Malo hercle vestro, confectores cardinum."   795

TAKE CARE, LUCILIUS, OR YOU MAY SPEND THE REST OF YOUR
DISDAINFUL DAYS IN A STATE OF CHRONIC UNDERNOURISHMENT.
TAKE ON A TASK THAT WILL PROVIDE YOU PRAISE AND PUT A
PROFIT IN YOUR POCKET, TOO.

. . . A GEORGIC

I work my farm and sell a few verses.
As usual I'm long on words and short of cash.
But you say you've made feasible the harvest
of a money crop to fatten me and furnish me
with ease against the winter of my days.

Assets and ambition are, you add, a man's
truest marks: as much as he possesses,
as much as he is himself possessed, so much
the sum of his real worth. I'm worth

one farm, a thistle patch. Whatever the wind
doesn't whirl away, frost bites or the sun's
furnace burns with rays poured down

like puddled iron. I thresh a bit of grain,
press my sour grapes, and reap red ink.

I'm worth a poem or two, white lines perhaps,
dividing the air, making no impression.
And because I have been worth friendly words
and votes to you, you've coined me a job,

an assistant secretaryship. Just what
exchange do you propose. A chance to serve
writs, not to write verse? A chance to farm
taxes, not land? A chance to turn from tilling
earth and grafting vines to filling my purse,

and yours, with public fees? I'll sell
no privacy for gold. Nor for a title gilded
on a door will I disown the guiltless name
by which I've known myself since I was born.

Text

quam fastidiosum ac vescum vivere. 722

Hunc laborem sumas laudem qui tibi ac fructum ferat.

713

Si messes facis et Musas si vendis Lavernae,   564

"si argentes indiges."   829

Sic tu illos fructus quaeras, adversa hieme olim
quis uti possis ac delectare domi te.   586–587

Aurum atque ambitio specimen virtutis virique est.
Tantum habeas tantum ipse sies tantique habearis.

1194–1195

Stat sentibus fundus.

1158

Pars difflatur vento, pars autem obrigescit frigore.

654

Primum fulgit uti caldum e furnacibus ferrum.

318

potius quam non magno messe, non proba vindemia.

759

nec si paulo minus usurast magna adiutatus diu,

758

et amabat omnes; nam ut discrimen non facit
neque signat linea alba, . . .   957–958

Mihi quidem non persuadetur publiceis mutem meos.

647

Publicanus vero ut Asiae fiam, ut scripturarius
pro Lucilio, id ego nolo et uno hoc non muto omnia.

650–651

NOW, LUCILIUS, THAT YOUR INCISIVE TONGUE HAS SCORED
THE ART OF POETRY, ONE TYPE AFTER ANOTHER, IT WOULD
BE DISTINCTLY IDIOTIC FOR US NOT TO LET YOU DO EX-
ACTLY AS YOU LIKE.

Thank you, one and all. I'd like, if it were possible . . . But
you still don't understand the present state of poetry, nor the
difference between the art and what you think it ought to be.

. . . ON THE NATURE OF MY ART

My fellowmen, the luster of your worth, the glow
of your good health, these are qualities I'd hoped
would persevere in every word, would penetrate
each line of verse I'm granted power to make.

I'm not allowed to achieve the polish desired.

O your cares and patent cures! O the inanity
that riddles you! You're tragic or you're stubbornly
absurd. Truth turns your stomachs. You whine, you
always see mountains in molehills, you're sore losers.

I'm afraid you've forgotten something.

A poet's a brickmaker using nothing more than raw
materials at hand, common clay and chaff, straw
glued by dirt. Or he's an oyster in an r-less
month soaking up the mucky flavor of his riverbed.

He'd rather gulp inspiration's strong spirits.

I am who I am in my skinshell. Some things I
cannot do. Do you think I'll keep striving, mind
nearly blown, to gloss you with poem? My wits
still know what's *poétique*: lovers' (not law-) suits.

But out of my gorge my heart pushes acid.
My verse is a black, wretched craft.

Text

Nunc, Gai, quoniam incilans nos laedis vicissim,

1075

Plane stultitiae plenum est uti numquam id facias quod
velis.   1260

Gratia habetur utrisque, illisque tibique simitu.

1092

"Vellem cumprimis, fieri si forte potisset, . . .

19

Non haec quid valeat, quidve hoc intersit et illud,
cognoscis. Primum hoc quod dicimus esse 'poema.'

401–402

Rem, populi salutem fictis versibus Lucilius
quibus potest inpertit, totumque hoc studiose et sedulo.

791–792

ut si id quod concupisset non aptus foret,   862

O curas hominum! O quantum est in rebus inane!

2

Tristes difficiles sumus, fastidimus bonorum.

313

Muginamur molimur subducimur.   313

Metuam ut memoriam retineas. . . .   698

    Lateres qui ducit habet nihil amplius numquam
quam commune lutum ac paleas caenumque aceratum.

352–353

        Quid ergo si ostrea Cerco
cognorit fluvium limum ac caenum sapere ipsum? . . .

357–358

quantum haurire animus Musarum e fontibus gestit.

1061

Ego si, qui sum et quo folliculo nunc sum indutus, non
   queo. . . .   691

          Tu Lucilium
credis contenturum, cum me ruperim, summa omnia
fecerim?   763–765

Scit ποιήτικον esse, videt tunica et toga quid sit.

542

       Ego ubi quem ex praecordiis
ecfero versum,   670–671

    Exhalas tum acidos ex pectore ructus.   130

qui schedium fa⟨cio.⟩   1131

ONE PLAYWRIGHT
AND
TWO EPIGRAMMATISTS

CLOCKS

Hellfire to him who discovered hours!
Damnation to him who invented clocks
and crumbled our days into minutes!
Once, a belly was clock
enough, a sure alarm for any child.
When it struck time to eat,
we ate, unless the cupboards were bare.
Now, when it's time to eat,
we don't, unless the clock permits.
Now we always tick with hunger.
Houses and offices gorge on clocks
while we crawl gaunt from hunger.

> —after Aquilius,
> about 150 B.C.

Text

Ut illum di perdant, primus qui horas repperit,
quique adeo primus statuit hic solarium,
qui mihi comminuit misero articulatim diem.
Nam unum me puero venter erat solarium
multo omnium istorum optimum et verissimum;
ubivis monebat esse, nisi quom nil erat.
Nunc etiam quod est non estur, nisi soli libet;
itaque adeo iam oppletum oppidum est solariis,
maior pars populi iam aridi reptant fame.

WAKING INTUITIVELY

Waking intuitively in the rosegrey light of rising sun,
I turned, saw you arise sleepwarm from my heart's side.
And knew (plain Calvinistic conscience, hold your tongue!)
that man, here, breathing, is more beautiful than God.

> —after Q. Lutatius Catulus,
> consul 102 B.C.

Text

Constiteram exorientem Auroram forte salutans,
    cum subito a laeva Roscius exoritur.
pace mihi liceat, caelestes, dicere vestra:
    mortalis visust pulchrior esse deo.

TOWARD TRANSLATION OF AN ANCIENT
AND UNIMPORTANT SOUNDSTATEMENT
BY VALERIUS AEDITUUS

Dicere cum conor curam tibi, Pamphila, cordis,
quid mi abs te quaeram? verba labris abeunt,
per pectus manat subito subido mihi sudor: 100? B.C.
sic tacitus, subidus, dum pudeo, pereo.
Dicere to say to speak *cum conor* when I try *curam*
the care (c-consonants) *curam tibi* When I try to
tell you of the love, All-loving *Pamphilia,*
cordis of heart in my heart *quid* what *mi abs te*
I from you *quaeram* shall quest request What shall I
ask of you? *verba* verbs words terms *labris*
from lips *abeunt* are gone (alphabet *abs labris* ab-
eunt & beta-alph ver*ba* ah lover's sighs) The words
are absent from my lips they flee fly (fly sigh
try perhaps to emphasize) while *per pectus*
(p-pounding pulse) down chest breast (he? she? me?
whose voice? yes his) down chest *manat* there runs

subito subido mihi sudor (ooze of vowels & sudden
sssteam) Down my burning body runs a sudden sweat:
sic tacitus so, silent *subidus* smouldering *dum*
pudeo I am ashamed & *pereo* I perish die When
Dicere cum conor . . . tibi When I try to tell you
(nothing but an elegance of assonance verse flies
poem flees a tide of Anglo-Saxon rises when I)
When I try, love, to tell you all my love, Lord only
    knows I try,
what words to speak? Verbs nouns all sounds flee,
    mouth's dry,   A.D. 1971
pulse pounds, sudden burning sweats wet chest thighs,
    my tonguetied
silence tells you lies, I burn & love wordshy I
    love & die.

COMMENTARY

MYTHOS

Loci classici for Homer's references to singers and bards are intentionally omitted. Classicists will know immediately where to find Thamyris, Phemius, and the others. Nonpolyglots, however, may gain much satisfaction by conducting their own searches through Richmond Lattimore's somewhat prosaic translation of the *Iliad* (Chicago, 1951) and Robert Fitzgerald's often very beautiful version of the *Odyssey* (New York, 1961).

CELEBRATIONS

Naevius: "The Pioneers" and "Epitaph"

Reasonably literal translations of the lines used in making these two *plasmata* will serve to give an idea of the plastic method. The first is composed of not necessarily contiguous lines from Naevius's epic on the First Punic War, tragedies, and plays of uncertain dramatic mode. The second has been transmitted to us whole.

"THE PIONEERS"

After Anchises saw the birdomen in the sky,
the consecrated vessels were placed in order on the table
    of the Penates;
he sacrificed a beautiful gold victim.

> The wives of both
left Troy by night, their heads covered,
both crying many tears as they left.

> When they were going outdoors there with the gold,

> clean and pretty clothes made of gold and citrus-sweet

> They carry beautiful vases, gold cups.

> with full blouses and gold-striped tunics, soft, saffron
>> dresses and shrouds

> without an iron prod, just as cattle go to death, hand-led

> With spread sail, North Wind, carry me outward to a
>> nearby port!

> to broken mountains where winds crush the land

> where the hemisphere stands enclosed in curved blueness

> men wood-dwelling and unskilled in war

> and King Amulius raised his hands to the heavens and
>> thanked the gods
> Their path many men follow.

"EPITAPH"

If it's fitting that immortals' tears flow for mortal men,
flow tears from divine Camenae-eyes for Naevius the
poet. For, after he was delivered into Death's treasure
house, into oblivion sank the Romans' knowledge of the
Latin language.

Ennius:

"THE BROTHERS" are of course Romulus and Remus, and
their quarrel, according to Ennius, was whether to call the city
Roma or Remora. It seems to me that the two ancestral heroes

of Rome are the Latin incarnations of brothers and twins met elsewhere in ancient literature—Castor and Pollux, Cain and Abel. And might they not also be the two faces of the Mars-power that promises both the sustenance of life in its sway over sprouting crops and the ending of life in its guidance of war? And the two halves of a dim bloody recurrent memory—the nomadic hunter losing again and again in life to the settled sower of seeds?

"TO BE A MAN" is my translation of the loaded word *virtus*. Pale northern English doesn't have a proper equivalent. Spanish does—*machismo*. "ONE DAY OF WAR: IX, DUST:" The stanzas of the *plasma* are arranged in a Fibonacci series—1:1:2:3:5:8:etc.—in which the sum of the two immediately preceding members produces the next member. I have used the series as an illustration of the notion that Ennius could have used Pythagorean ratios to structure some of his work; after the first few intervals, dividing any member of the series by the one following it, will yield the Golden Mean—.618.

POSSIBILITIES

Lucilius:

". . . A LETTER:" Apologies to Rimbaud. I've tampered with a line from his *"Adieu," A Season in Hell* in order to translate the Greek line that Lucilius pilfered from the *Odyssey* XI, 491. In the *Odyssey* Odysseus, visiting Hades, is told by Agamemnon's shade that the late hero would rather be alive and poor than made high king over dead men.

"S." Marcus Pacuvius (220?–130? B.C.), son of Ennius's sister, was a painter and writer of tragedies that enjoyed great popularity during and after his lifetime. Cicero admired his style. Lucilius definitely did not and parodied Pacuvian polysyllables and bombast. With some justification. The verse form used for the *plasma* is the double dactyl, invented by the poets John Hollander and Anthony Hecht.

Aquilius:

"clocks:" Nobody seems to know anything about Aquilius other than that such a name is attached to this fragment from a comedy. He may actually have been Plautus. It doesn't matter. The fragment stands on its own feet.

SOURCES
AND RESOURCES

READINGS OF HISTORY:

1. J. W. Duff, *A Literary History of Rome: From the Origins to the Close of the Golden Age*, 2d ed. (New York: Charles Scribner's Sons, 1928), p. 79. *Locus classicus* from Theodor Mommsen, *The History of Rome*, trans. by William Purdie Dickson. Everyman's Library. (London: J. M. Dent & Sons Ltd., n.d.). vol. 1, p. 454.

2. *The Oxford Book of Latin Verse: From the Earliest Fragments to the End of the Vth Century A.D.*, ed. by H. W. Garrod (Oxford, 1912), p. 2. *Locus classicus* provided by James Hynd, Department of Classics, The University of Texas, Austin.

3. *Remains of Old Latin*, ed. and trans. by E. H. Warmington. Loeb Classical Library. (Cambridge, Massachusetts: Harvard University Press, 1961), vol. 2, p. 272.

4. *Remains*, vol. 2, p. 62, and the same, vol. 3, p. 36, respectively.

5. The numbers of the Lucilian and Ennian passages quoted in this essay are those assigned by Warmington, *Remains*, vols. 2 and 1.

6. *Feeling and Form* (New York: Charles Scribner's Sons, 1953), pp. 40, 212, and 253, respectively.

7. *The Seamless Web* (New York: George Braziller, 1970), pp. 10–14, especially.

8. "Stress and Behavior," *Scientific American*, vol. 224, no. 1 (January 1971).

9. Burnshaw, work cited, p. 24.

10. Robert Graves, *The Greek Myths* (Baltimore, Maryland: Penguin Books, 1955), vol. 1, p. 360. Graves also identifies Egeria as an oak-queen in *The White Goddess* (New York, 1948), pp. 191 and 293.

11. Sir James George Frazer, *The Golden Bough: A Study in Magic*

and *Religion,* abridged ed. (New York: The Macmillan Company, 1951), pp. 4, 9, 169–170, and 175.

12. Graves, *The Greek Myths,* vol. 1, p. 289; *The White Goddess,* p. 191.

13. Varro, quoted by Aulus Gellius, *Noctium Atticarum,* XVI.xvi.4.

14. *The Mind of Primitive Man,* rev. ed. (New York: The Macmillan Company, 1938), pp. 198–200.

15. *La pensée sauvage* (Paris, 1962), pp. 5–24.

16. *Play, Dreams and Imitation in Childhood (La formation du symbole),* trans. by C. Gattegno and F. M. Hodgson (New York: W. W. Norton & Company, 1962), pp. 197–198.

17. Suzanne K. Langer, *Philosophy in a New Key* (New York: The New American Library, 1951), pp. 130–131.

18. Bärbel Inhelder and Jean Piaget, *The Growth of Logical Thinking from Childhood to Adolescence,* trans. by Anne Parsons and Stanley Milgram (New York: Basic Books, Inc., 1958), p. 48.

19. The same, p. 343.

20. Jane Ellen Harrison, *Themis: A Study of the Social Origins of Greek Religion* (New Hyde Park, New York: University Books, 1962), pp. 194–195.

21. The same, p. 196.

22. *The Oxford Classical Dictionary* (Oxford, 1953), p. 370.

23. W. Warde Fowler, *The Roman Festivals of the Period of the Republic: An Introduction to the Study of the Religion of the Romans* (London: Macmillan and Co., Limited, 1899), pp. 73–74.

24. *The Oxford Book of Latin Verse,* p. 512.

25. Harrison, work cited, p. 204.

26. The same, pp. 31 ff.

27. Sir Arthur Grimble, *Return to the Islands: Life and Legend in the Gilberts* (New York: William Morrow & Co., 1957), p. 200.

28. *Remains,* vol. 2, pp. 474, 478–480, and 474, respectively.

29. The same, vol. 4, Epitaph 10, p. 8.

30. Pseudo-Sallust, *ad Caesarem de Republica,* I.i.2, as quoted by Duff, work cited, p. 89.

31. Priscian, as quoted by Duff, the same, place cited.

32. Alberto Grilli, *Studi enniani* (Paideia-Brescia, n.d.), p. 136.

33. John Hollander, *The Untuning of the Sky: Ideas of Music in English Poetry, 1500–1700* (Princeton, New Jersey: Princeton University Press, 1961), p. 13.

34. George E. Duckworth, *Structural Patterns and Proportions in Vergil's* Aeneid: *A Study in Mathematical Composition* (Ann Arbor: The University of Michigan Press, 1962), pp. 77, 97–98, and 104.

BRONZE TEXT: EPIGRAPH

Quintilian, Loeb Classical Library (1933), vol. 1.

BRONZE TEXTS: SURVIVAL

THE SALIAN HYMNS:

1. Varro, *de Lingua Latina*, IX.61. Loeb Classical Library (1938), vol. 1.
2. *The Oxford Book of Latin Verse*, p. 1.
3. Ovid, *Fasti*, III.390. Loeb Classical Library (1959).

THE ARVAL CHANT: *The Oxford Book of Latin Verse*, pp. 1–2.

IRON TEXTS: EPIGRAPH

Livius Andronicus: *Remains of Old Latin*, Loeb Classical Library (1961), vol. 2.

IRON TEXTS: CELEBRATION

Naevius: *Remains*, vol. 2.
Ennius: *Remains*, vol. 1, except for italicized words and phrases that were suggested by Otto Skutsch. The first line of text for "Evocation" will be found in his book *Studia Enniana* (London, 1968), p. 3. The passage, *Annales* 80–100, used as a text for "The Brothers," follows Professor Skutsch's emendations, work cited, pp. 62–81. The unnumbered word *Vesper*, last line of text for "X: Evening," will be found in *Remains*, vol. 1, p. 563.
Anonymous Epitaph: *Remains*, vol. 4, p. 12.

IRON TEXTS: POSSIBILITIES

Naevius: *Remains*, vol. 2.
Lucilius: *Remains*, vol. 3. Unnumbered words and phrases, used as texts for ". . . On Natural History, 5," ". . . On Natural History, 6," and "Lucilius, Please Entertain Us," will be found in the same volume, pp. 420, 419, and 420, respectively.
Aquilius: Aulus Gellius, *Noctium Atticarum*, III.iii.5. Loeb Classical Library (1961), vol. 1.
Q. Lutatius Catulus: *The Oxford Book of Latin Verse*, p. 23.
Valerius Aedituus: Gellius, work cited, XIX.ix.11. Loeb, vol. 3.

BIBLIOGRAPHY

Alföldi, Andrew. *Early Rome and the Latins.* Ann Arbor: The University of Michigan Press, 1963.

Aristotle. *Theory of Poetry and Fine Art,* trans. and with critical notes by S. H. Butcher, 4th ed. New York: Dover Publications, Inc., 1951.

Auden, W. H. *Secondary Worlds.* New York: Random House, 1968.

Blake, William. "Hear the voice of the Bard!", *The Oxford Book of English Verse, 1250–1900,* ed. by Arthur Quiller-Couch. Oxford, 1915.

Bloch, Raymond. *The Origins of Rome.* New York: Frederick A. Praeger, 1960.

Boas, Franz. *The Mind of Primitive Man,* rev. ed. New York: The Macmillan Company, 1938.

Bourlière, François, and others. *The Land and Wildlife of Eurasia.* New York: Time, Incorporated, 1964.

Bowra, C. M. *Primitive Song.* Cleveland and New York: The World Publishing Company, 1962.

Bulfinch, Thomas. *The Age of Fable,* with notes, revisions, and additions by William H. Klapp. Philadelphia: Henry Altemus Co., 1903.

Burnshaw, Stanley. *The Seamless Web.* New York: George Braziller, 1970.

Campbell, Joseph. *The Masks of God: Primitive Mythology.* New York: The Viking Press, 1959.

Cato. *de Re Rustica,* trans. by William Davis Hooper. Loeb Classical Library. Cambridge, Massachusetts: Harvard University Press, 1934.

Catullus, ed. by Elmer Truesdale Merrill. Boston: Ginn and Company, 1893.

Chadwick, H. Munro, and N. Kershaw Chadwick. *The Growth of*

Literature: Vol. 1, The Ancient Literatures of Europe. Cambridge, 1932.

———. The Growth of Literature: Vol. 3, Part IV, "A General Survey." New York: The Macmillan Company, 1940.

Cicero. ad Quintum Fratrem: Dialogi Tres de Oratore, cum excerptis ex notis variorum. Novi-Portum: H. Howe & Soc., 1836.

Cornelison, Ann. Torregreca: Life, Death, Miracles. Boston: Little, Brown and Company, 1969.

Curran, Leo C. "Gellius and the Lover's Pallor: A Note on Catullus 80," Arion 5.1 (Spring 1966).

Dionysius of Halicarnassus. Roman Antiquities, trans. by Earnest Cary. Loeb Classical Library. Cambridge, Massachusetts: Harvard University Press, 1960. Vol. 1.

Duckworth, George E. Structural Patterns and Proportions in Vergil's Aeneid: A Study in Mathematical Composition. Ann Arbor: The University of Michigan Press, 1962.

Duff, John Wight. A Literary History of Rome: From the Origins to the Close of the Golden Age, 2d ed. New York: Charles Scribner's Sons, 1928.

———. Roman Satire: Its Outlook on Social Life. Hamden, Connecticut: Archon Press, 1964.

Durand, John D. "Mortality Estimates from Roman Tombstone Inscriptions," American Journal of Sociology, vol. 65 (1960), pp. 365–373.

Flavius Vopiscus. "Divus Aurelianus," Scriptores Historiae Augustae, trans. by David Magie. Loeb Classical Library. Cambridge, Massachusetts: Harvard University Press, 1961. Vol. 3.

Fowler, W. Warde. The Roman Festivals of the Period of the Republic: An Introduction to the Study of the Religion of the Romans. London: Macmillan and Company, Limited, 1899.

Frank, Tenney. Life and Literature in the Roman Republic. Berkeley and Los Angeles: University of California Press, 1930.

Frazer, Sir James George. The Golden Bough: A Study in Magic and Religion, abr. ed. New York: The Macmillan Company, 1951.

Frost, Robert. "The Figure a Poem Makes," Complete Poems of Robert Frost. New York: Holt, Rinehart and Winston, Inc., 1949.

———. In the Clearing. New York: Holt, Rinehart and Winston, 1962.

Gardner, Martin. "Phi: The Golden Ratio," The 2nd Scientific American Book of Mathematical Puzzles and Diversions. New York: Simon and Schuster, 1961.

Gayley, Charles Mills, ed. The Classic Myths in English Literature. Boston: Ginn & Company, 1897.

Gellius, Aulus. *Noctium Atticarum,* trans. by John C. Rolfe. Loeb Classical Library. Cambridge, Massachusetts: Harvard University Press, 1961. 3 vols.

Gjerstad, Einar. *Early Rome: Vol. 2, The Tombs.* Lund, 1956.

Graves, Robert. *The Greek Myths.* Baltimore, Maryland: Penguin Books, 1955. 2 vols.

————. *The White Goddess: A Historical Grammar of Poetic Myth.* New York: Creative Age Press, 1948.

Grilli, Alberto. *Studi enniani.* Paideia-Brescia, n.d.

Grimble, Sir Arthur. *Return to the Islands: Life and Legend in the Gilberts.* New York: William Morrow & Co., 1957.

Gummere, Francis B. *The Beginnings of Poetry.* New York: The Macmillan Company, 1901.

Hadas, Moses. *Ancilla to Classical Reading.* New York: Columbia University Press, 1954.

Halporn, James W., Martin Ostwald, and Thomas G. Rosenmeyer. *The Meters of Greek and Latin Poetry.* Indianapolis and New York: The Bobbs-Merrill Company, Inc., 1963.

Hamilton, Edith. *The Roman Way.* New York: W. W. Norton Company, Inc., 1932.

Harrison, Jane Ellen. *Epilegomena to the Study of Greek Religion and Themis: A Study of the Social Origins of Greek Religion.* New Hyde Park, New York: University Books, 1962.

Helm, E. Eugene. "The Vibrating String of the Pythagoreans," *Scientific American,* vol. 217, no. 6 (December 1967), pp. 92–103.

Hesiod. *Theogony* and *Works and Days,* trans. by Hugh G. Evelyn-White. Loeb Classical Library. Cambridge, Massachusetts: Harvard University Press, 1943.

Highet, Gilbert. *Juvenal the Satirist: A Study.* Oxford, 1954.

Hodge, Henry. *Technology in the Ancient World.* New York: Alfred A. Knopf, 1970.

Hoffer, Eric. *The Ordeal of Change.* New York: Harper and Row, 1963.

Hollander, John, and Anthony Hecht, eds. *Jiggery-Pokery: A Compendium of Double Dactyls.* New York: Atheneum, 1967.

Hollander, John. *The Untuning of the Sky: Ideas of Music in English Poetry, 1500–1700.* Princeton, New Jersey: Princeton University Press, 1961.

Homer. *Iliad, trans.* and with an introduction by Richmond Lattimore. Chicago: The University of Chicago Press, 1951.

————. *Odyssey,* trans. by Robert Fitzgerald. New York: Doubleday Anchor Books, 1961.

Hooke, S. H. *Middle Eastern Mythology*. Baltimore, Maryland: Penguin Books, 1961.

Horace. *Satires, Epistles, and Ars Poetica*, trans. by H. Rushton Fairclough. Loeb Classical Library. Cambridge, Massachusetts: Harvard University Press, 1966.

Housman, A. E. *The Name and Nature of Poetry*. New York: The Macmillan Company, 1937.

Hughes, Ted. *Crow*. New York: Harper & Row, Publishers, 1971.

Inhelder, Bärbel, and Jean Piaget. *The Growth of Logical Thinking from Childhood to Adolescence*, trans. by Anne Parsons and Stanley Milgram. New York: Basic Books, Inc., 1958.

Kitto, H. D. F. *Poiesis: Structure and Thought*. Berkeley and Los Angeles: University of California Press, 1966.

Langer, Suzanne K. *Feeling and Form*. New York: Charles Scribner's Sons, 1953.

————. *Philosophical Sketches: A Study of the Human Mind in Relation to Feeling, Explored through Art, Language, and Symbol*. Baltimore, Maryland: The Johns Hopkins Press, 1962.

————. *Philosophy in a New Key*. Cambridge, Massachusetts: Harvard University Press, 1951.

Lesky, Albin. *A History of Greek Literature*, 2d ed., trans by James Willis and Cornelius de Heer. New York: Thomas Y. Crowell Company, 1963.

Lévi-Strauss, Claude. *La pensée sauvage*. Paris: Librarie Plon, 1962.

Levine, Seymour. "Stress and Behavior," *Scientific American*, vol. 224, no. 1 (January 1971), pp. 26–31.

Lewis, Richard, ed. *Miracles: Poems by Children of the English-speaking World*. New York: Simon and Schuster, 1966.

————. *Out of the Earth I Sing: Poetry and Songs of Primitive Peoples of the World*. New York: W. W. Norton & Company, Inc., 1968.

Lifton, Robert Jay. *History and Human Survival*. New York: Random House, 1970.

Livy. *ab Urbe Condita*, trans. by B. O. Foster. Loeb Classical Library. Cambridge, Massachusetts: Harvard University Press, 1967, 1960, and 1960. Vols. 1–3.

Maiuri, Amadeo. *Roman Painting*. Geneva: Editions Albert Skira, 1953.

Malinowski, Bronislaw. *Sex, Culture, and Myth*. New York: Harcourt, Brace & World, Inc., 1962.

Mench, Fred. "Film Sense in the *Aeneid*," *Arion* 8.3 (Autumn 1969).

Mommsen, Theodor. *The History of Rome*, trans. by William Purdie Dickson. Everyman's Library. London: J. M. Dent & Sons Ltd., n.d. 4 vols.

Opie, Iona, and Peter Opie, eds. *The Oxford Nursery Rhyme Book.* New York and Oxford: Oxford University Press, 1955.

Otis, Brooks. "The Uniqueness of Latin Literature," *Arion* 6.2 (Summer 1967).

Ovid. *Fasti,* trans. by Sir James George Frazer. Loeb Classical Library. Cambridge, Massachusetts: Harvard University Press, 1959.

The Oxford Book of Latin Verse: From the Earliest Fragments to the End of the Vth Century A.D., ed. by H. W. Garrod. Oxford, 1912.

The Oxford Classical Dictionary. Oxford, 1953.

Pausanias. *Description of Greece,* trans. by W. H. S. Jones. Loeb Classical Library. London: William Heinemann, 1918–1935. 5 vols.

Perowne, Stewart. *Death of the Roman Republic: From 146 B.C. to the Birth of the Roman Empire.* New York: Doubleday & Company, Inc., 1968.

Persius. *Juvenal and Persius,* trans. by G. G. Ramsay. Loeb Classical Library. Cambridge, Massachusetts: Harvard University Press, 1957.

Piaget, Jean. *Play, Dreams and Imitation in Childhood,* trans. by C. Gattegno and F. M. Hodgson. New York: W. W. Norton & Company, Inc., 1962.

Plato. *The Republic,* ed. with critical notes, commentary and appendices by James Adam. Cambridge, 1965. 2 vols.

Pliny. *Natural History,* trans. by W. H. S. Jones. Loeb Classical Library. London: William Heinemann Ltd., 1963. Vol. 8.

Pritchard, James Bennett, ed. *Ancient Near Eastern Texts Relating to the Old Testament,* 2d ed. Princeton, New Jersey: Princeton University Press, 1955.

Quintilian. *Institutio Oratoria,* trans. by H. E. Butler. Loeb Classical Library. New York: G. P. Putnam's Sons, 1933. Vols. 1–3.

Remains of Old Latin, ed. and trans. by E. H. Warmington. Loeb Classical Library. Cambridge, Massachusetts: Harvard University Press, 1961. 4 vols.

Rimbaud, introduced and ed. by Oliver Bernard. Baltimore, Maryland: Penguin Books, 1962.

Sandys, Sir John Edwin. *A Companion to Latin Studies,* 3d ed. New York: Hafner Publishing Co., 1968.

Sextus Empiricus, trans. by R. G. Bury. Loeb Classical Library. Cambridge, Massachusetts: Harvard University Press, 1949. Vol. 4.

Shapiro, Harry L., ed. *Man, Culture, and Society.* A Galaxy Book. New York: Oxford University Press, 1960.

Skutsch, Otto. *Studia Enniana*. London: The Athlone Press, 1968.

Sondheim, Steven. *A Funny Thing Happened on the Way to the Forum*. New York: Dodd, Mead and Company, 1963.

Stevens, Wallace. *The Collected Poems of Wallace Stevens*. New York: Alfred A. Knopf, 1954.

Suetonius. *de Vita Caesarum: Libri I–II*, with introduction and notes by John Howell Westcott and Edwin Moore Rankin. Boston: Allyn and Bacon, 1918.

Tanner, J. M. "Earlier Maturation in Man," *Scientific American*, vol. 218, no. 1 (January 1968), pp. 21–27.

Trask, Willard R., ed. *The Unwritten Song: Poetry of the Primitive and Traditional Peoples of the World*. New York: The Macmillan Company, vol. 1 1966, vol. 2 1967.

Varro. *de Lingua Latina*, trans. by Roland G. Kent. Loeb Classical Library. London: William Heinemann Ltd., 1938. 2 vols.

———. *Rerum Rusticarum*, trans. by William Davis Hooper. Loeb Classical Library. Cambridge, Massachusetts: Harvard University Press, 1934.

Wheeler, Arthur Leslie. *Catullus and the Traditions of Ancient Poetry*. Berkeley, California: University of California Press, 1934.

White, C. Langdon, and George T. Renner. *Human Geography: An Ecological Study of Society*. New York: Appleton-Century-Crofts, Inc., 1948.

Wills, Gary, ed. *Roman Culture: Weapons and the Man*. New York: George Braziller, 1966.

Wordsworth, J. *Fragments and Specimens of Early Latin*. Oxford, 1874.

dixi. abei.

INDEX

(Italicized page numbers refer to translations or *plasmata*.)

censorship of, 7, 57
change from bronze to iron, 51–57
evolution of, 15–18
experimentation in, 17, 62, 69, 75–76
as performing art, 7, 15, 25, 56
resources of, 63, 69
shift of emphasis in, 9, 15, 77
uses of, 5, 7, 17, 25, 41–42, 52, 57, 58–59, 78
See also Bronze poetry; Iron poetry
ποιητής, 22, 41
Pompey the Great, 73
Pope, Alexander, 76
Porcius Licinus, 5
Possibility, poetry of, 15, 17–18, 48–51, 56, 58, 69–70, 73–77, 125–166, 169–170
Postvorta, 23, 24
Pound, Ezra, 6, 62, 76
Practical connection. See Connections
Prayers, 3
Predatory economics, 53, 70
Prelogical thought. See Thought
Priests, 16, 24–25, 30–31, 32, 42–44, 45, 53, 66. See also Arval Brothers; Salian priests
Primitive thought. See Thought
Propertius, 76
Prophecies, 3
Prophet, 16, 24, 25, 41. See also Vates
Proverbs, 3
Punic War, First, 5, 53, 64, 65, 167; Second, 65, 71
Pythagorean ideas, 66–68
Pythagorean ratios, 67, 68, 169
Pythagoras, 66–67

Quintilian, 44, 60

Religio, 32
Religion, 4, 23, 24, 25, 32–33, 38, 42, 43–44, 48, 52, 53, 54, 58, 77
Remus, 46, 168
Republic, 9, 30, 38, 54–57, 58, 70–73, 76
Rimbaud, Arthur, 169
Roman Games, 5

Romanitas, 64, 69
Romulus, 23, 38, 39, 46, 64, 168

Sacer, 24
Salian hymns, 4–5, 23, 25–27, 32–41, 44, 77, 83–84
Salian priests, 4, 12, 20, 23, 25, 26–27, 33, 35–37, 40–41, 43–44
Saliare, 27
Samuel, I, quoted, 50
Satire, 3, 6, 18, 51, 65, 70, 73–75, 76, 126–163
Satura and saturae, 51, 73, 74
Saturnian meter, 5, 6, 8, 46, 55, 58, 63, 64, 70
Scipio Aemilianus, 73
Scipio Africanus, 65
Scipio Hispanus, Gnaeus Cornelius, 47
Sextus Empiricus, 10, 60
Singer, 3, 20–21, 23, 33, 34, 36, 44, 50, 51, 52, 55, 69, 77, 167
Singers' guild, 20
Stevens, Wallace, 12; quoted, 36
Stress, 13, 68
Style, 57, 75, 76
Suetonius, 49
Survival, poetry of, 15–16, 22–45, 47, 52, 56, 58, 74, 83–86
Symbol and symbols, 15, 35, 39, 68
Symbolic connection. See Connections
Symbolic thought. See Thought
Symbolization of feeling, 12, 14, 44, 76

Table graces, 3
Terence, 5, 6
Terpsichore, 19, 20
Thamyris, 21, 167
Thought:
    archaic, 27–37
    domestic, 27, 28
    prelogical, 27, 34–36
    primitive, 27–33
    "scientific," 28
    symbolic, 35
Tradition, 3, 42, 52, 53, 55, 57, 71
Traditional ideas, 27–32
Traditional materials, 24, 28, 43
Tragedy, 3, 5, 38, 56, 57, 58, 64, 65, 66, 73, 80, 167, 169